The Perfect Prayer

The Perfect Prayer

Search for the Kingdom through the Lord's Prayer

Philip Mathias

MINNEAPOLIS

THE PERFECT PRAYER
Search for the Kingdom through the Lord's Prayer

Copyright © 2005 Philip Mathias. All rights reserved. Except for brief quotations in critical articles or reviews, no part of this book may be reproduced in any manner without prior written permission from the publisher. Write to: Permissions, Augsburg Fortress, Box 1209, Minneapolis, MN 55440.

Large-quantity purchases or custom editions of this book are available at a discount from the publisher. For more information, contact the sales department at Augsburg Fortress, Publishers, 1-800-328-4648, or write to: Sales Director, Augsburg Fortress, Publishers, P. O. Box 1209, Minneapolis, MN 55440-1209.

Unless otherwise noted, Scripture passages are from the New Revised Standard Version of the Bible, copyright © 1946, 1952, 1971, 1989 by the Division of Christian Education of the National Council of the Churches of Christ in the USA. Used by permission.

ISBN 0-8066-5156-3

Cover design by Kevin Van der Leek, cover photo credit: Réunion des Musées Nationaux/ Art Resource, New York
Book design by Phoenix Type

The paper used in this publication meets the minimum requirements of American National Standard for Information Sciences—Permanence of Paper for Printed Library Materials, ANSI Z329.48-1984. ∞ ™

Manufactured in Canada

09   08   07   06   05   1   2   3   4   5   6   7   8   9   10

Contents

Introduction　xi

1. The Prayer　1
2. Father　20
3. Hallowed Be Thy Name　45
4. Thy Kingdom Come　71
5. The Other Side　98
6. Give Us This Day Our Daily Bread　101
7. And Forgive Us Our Sins;
   We Too Forgive All Those Who Trespass Against Us　123
8. And Lead Us Not into Temptation　138
9. The Power of the Prayer　151

Notes　155

Acknowledgments

My good friend, Ken Westhues, who is Professor of Sociology at the University of Waterloo, magnanimously gave me his encouragement and support at a time when my confidence in this book was wavering. Peter Orme, an Anglican priest in Toronto, nudged me into some better theological insights, while allowing me to believe they were the fruits of my own inspiration. My old friend Don Rumball saw merit in an early version of this book that others suggested I abandon. I would also like to thank my friend and agent Nick Harris for his stubborn hard work on my behalf. But most of all, I would like to acknowledge the enormous support given by my wife Caroline at all times.

*For Alex,
James, and
Carol*

Introduction

This book explores the core of Christian joy—the search for the kingdom of God. It does so through the lens of the prayer Jesus gave to his disciples, the one we call the Lord's Prayer or the Our Father. This magnificent prayer is composed of six petitions, each rich with vibrant meaning. This book explores the role each petition plays in the fulfillment of the prayer's high aspiration—the coming of the kingdom of God. The prayer is also examined as a whole, because it is much greater than the sum of its parts in the way that a symphony is more than a collection of musical notes.

The basis for this book is the shorter version of Jesus's prayer, the one found in Luke's Gospel. Although this is considered an archaic curiosity by many, it is far superior for literary analysis and contemplation than the better known prayer found in Matthew, which is more fruitful for communal recitation. But both versions carry the highest values of Christianity and its theology at their very core.

Christianity is not a rock-hard obligation that damns people who do not accept it, as some would like us to believe. Christianity is not an iron prison filled with a brilliant light in which we must lock ourselves up and "sunbathe in the divine presence" or face the consequences. Christianity is not even a theological system that has been proven true beyond a reasonable doubt. Christianity is a powerful persuasion, and for those who are persuaded it is a wonderful secret. It is the free choice of a blessing understood and accepted, one that plumps up into an enthusiastic way of life. Christianity is a gift received and a gift returned. Many people do not receive the gift, so they cannot return it. Others receive the gift and are genuinely unable to pass it on for the most valid of reasosns. None of these people are lesser people for all that. All this is found in the Lord's Prayer.

In my view, the core of Christianity is never guilt and rectitude. It is never the certainty of black and white theology. It is the stubborn search for the kingdom of God, which involves heroism and sacrifice, and above all, the exhilaration of a journey into the unknown, ending in a marvelous discovery. Seeking the kingdom is an enormous risk, and yet it brings the greatest of all security. It is the finest celebration of human life, though it is founded on a prayerful austerity. It is the spring of the world and the summer of the spirit. It is the joyful discovery of what everybody is looking for, whether they are aware of it or not, and that is the exaltation of their humanity. It is this search for the kingdom, through Jesus's perfect prayer, that this books seeks to document, though incompletely and inadequately.

The text quotes Jesus through the gospels many times, as it must. It does not take into account the conclusions of the Jesus Project, which allegedly applies "scientific analysis" to determine what Jesus did and did not say. "Science" always places itself under severe limitations when considering questions of faith or spirituality or ethics, because these engage all our humanity, not just our powers of observation and reason. Scientific conclusions are also rooted in a particular time, and almost always change in big or small ways. A preoccupation with the shifting sands of science kills the search for the kingdom before it is even begun.

This book comes to the obvious conclusion that God is neither male nor female. But I have consistently referred to God as "he" or "him." The reason is entirely linguistic. I have not found a way to use the English language to express this notion of the divine super-gender without clumsiness and confusion, both of which would obscure the ideas and conclusions that I have tried to present. Alternating "he" and "she" doesn't work because it is too arch and would force the gender issue into every single reference to God. Referring to God as "it" doesn't work either for obvious reasons. Using no pronouns at all and referring only to "God" as "God" each time is enormously heavy-handed and would greatly belabor the text. Thus the misleading "he" seems to be the only literary solution that works.

Finally, I would like the reader to know that I have no formal qualifications to present to him or her for their comfort while reading this book. I have never systematically studied theology, and I am not a particularly devotional person. What I am is a practiced writer who has spent forty-one years as a journalist and has given much thought to the questions in this book. In that sense, this book is literary rather than learned. It respects scholarship, but makes no attempt to contribute to it. I shall be delighted if it provokes a little thought.

1

The Prayer

—

Father,
Hallowed be thy name;
Thy kingdom come;
Give us this day our daily bread;
And forgive us our sins; we too forgive all those who trespass against us;
And lead us not into temptation.

Luke 11:2-4[1]

This lovely spoken "hymn" was composed by Jesus for his disciples on the spur of the moment one day after one of them said, "Lord, teach us how to pray." This version from Luke's Gospel consists of only thirty-five words, all of which can be understood by a child. Yet, this is one of the most powerful pieces of literature ever written in any language or any culture. It is a poetic diamond that sends worlds of light shining through its six polished facets from the brilliance that glows bright within. It has been the subject of hundreds of books, from the fourth-century sermons of Gregory of Nyssa,[2] to a tribute by twentieth-century theologian Leonardo Boff,[3] as well as hundreds of other works of veneration and scholarship in all ages. But even after two thousand years of reflection, this exquisite homily on the spiritual life still yields fresh insights. Its literary and spiritual reach goes far beyond any human genius. It is the perfect guide in the search for the mysterious kingdom of God.

First and foremost, this is a prayer—a series of six petitions that embody everything we should ever say to God at any time. It is also a mantra to calm the heavy heart. But it is richer in healing than all the great Hindu chants and the secret formulas of the transcendentalists, which are paper-thin by comparison. This prayer confirms, for all who consult it, that the kingdom of God is a place of good health in body, spirit, and soul.

Beyond that, this prayer is also a crash course in theology. Deep within its beautiful brevity, it contains a rich appreciation of the whole sweep of God's revelation—from the story of Adam and Eve to the resurrection of Jesus. A tight kinship can be found, for example, between these thirty-five words and the Ten Commandments. Jesus's prayer embraces this antique catalog of forbidden deeds, and builds upon them to construct a vibrant spirituality that rises high above the Law, the way a skyscraper rises from its foundations.

Finally, Jesus's prayer reveals who God is, what we are, how we became alienated from God, and the consequences of all this moral chaos. The prayer delivers razor-sharp insights into our battered spirituality and ends that dreary tale of sin and suffering with a triumph—a vision of our reconciliation with God in the coming of his kingdom.

What Is Prayer?

Prayer consumes the whole person—the spirit, the heart, and the body. It is a total engagement with God, and with the community at large, in the light of God's wishes. Like all human endeavors, prayer is often poorly practiced. The petitioner may be distracted or tired and mumble the words out of a sense of duty, with little attention to meaning. The prayer may also be aimed short of God, into the grasp of St. Blaise or St. Jude or St. Benedict, who are asked to intercede with God on our behalf, a practice that may have its roots in ancient protocol, when a commoner could only petition a king through a courtier. Praying to saints may also cover the petitioner's self-imagined inadequacy, or real sinfulness.

Prayer can still be less than perfect even when it is directed single-mindedly to God himself. Prayer is self-centered when it asks God for one's own needs—perhaps a car or a raise. Prayer is elitist when it contemplates the divine mysteries, but shows little interest in the rest of humanity. Here, the image comes to mind of a military leader in his white uniform, eyes fixed on the altar, while his troops brutalize the people. Even sincere, selfless prayer lacks its full potential when it is addressed to "God," which is only the deity's name; or to "the Creator," which describes what God has accomplished; or to the "Lord," which is his high status within the community. Jesus says we must address God as "the Father," which is his loving relationship with all people, as well as his rightful title as the progenitor of every person and every thing.

The Lord's Prayer is the perfect prayer. It is directed toward God himself as our loving Father. And it prays first that God the Father's own wishes will be met—that he will be honored among the nations, and that he will be accepted as the eternal King. But these are also prayers for our own well-being. When we hallow God's name and seek his kingdom, we exalt ourselves into the highest state of our humanity. Thus exalted, we ask God for security—at the material level by "Give us . . . bread"; at the psychological level by "Forgive us our trespasses"; and at the spiritual level by "And lead us not into temptation." We know these petitions will be answered, so the prayer transforms itself from a chain of requests into a single divine benediction.

The Two Prayers

The first step in any journey of appreciation of this prayer is to place the two versions—Luke's and Matthew's—side by side and compare them, because each has its own special riches that mirror the way in which the prayer was delivered. Matthew's version was brought forth on a public occasion, before a crowd of Jesus's followers, during the Sermon on the Mount. Matthew gives us more than Luke, adapting Jesus's prayer to public worship. Luke's version was delivered when only the disciples were gathered around Jesus. And Luke's version (at the opening of this chapter) is more rewarding to contemplation in private. Each version gains something, and loses something, by the form in which it is presented.

Matthew's version of the Lord's Prayer is the most familiar.

Our Father who art in heaven,
Hallowed be thy name;
Thy kingdom come;
Thy will be done,

On earth as it is in heaven.
Give us this day our daily bread;
And forgive us our trespasses,
As we forgive them that trespass against us;
And lead us not into temptation,
But deliver us from evil.

Matthew 6:9-13
(See footnote #1)

This rendition contains three phrases that were added, either by Matthew or by the early Christians. This embellishment renders Matthew's version both mellifluous and easier to recite aloud.

Here is a comparison:

Luke	Matthew
Father	**Our** Father **who art in heaven**
Hallowed be thy name	Hallowed be thy name
Thy Kingdom come	Thy Kingdom come
—	**Thy will be done,** **On earth as it is in heaven**
Give us this day our daily bread	Give us this day our daily bread
And forgive us our sins; we too forgive all those who trespass against us.	And forgive us our trespasses, as we forgive them that trespass against us.
And lead us not into temptation.	And lead us not into temptation
—	**But deliver us from evil. Amen**

In Matthew's rendering, the words "Our Father who art in heaven" make the prayer flow more fluidly than Luke's bald beginning—"Father." And Matthew's words do run sweetly. "Our Father who art in heaven, Hallowed be thy name. Thy kingdom come..." The person praying is bathed in a beautiful piety with the rest of the congregation while reciting the prayer, easily and devoutly. Matthew also inserts "Thy will be done, On earth as it is in heaven" in the middle of the prayer. This passage comes from a powerful prayer of spiritual surrender made by Jesus on another occasion: "Father... thy will be done!" (Matthew 26:42). In saying "Thy will be done" in Matthew's prayer, we sink into the peace of allowing God to decide what is best. Matthew then inserts, "But deliver us from evil" at the end. These words also enhance the prayer's rhythm for public recital by nicely rounding off the end. They also reinforce the idea of the totality of God's protection. "Lord, don't only lead us away from temptation but deliver us from evil always."

But each particle added by Matthew weakens the prayer's power. "Our Father," for example, is more artificial than Luke's simple "Father." That's because "Our Father" is not a natural way to speak to a parent. Even if the child speaks on behalf of brothers and sisters standing nearby, he would never call out "Our Father, can we go out to play?" or "Our Mother, can we have a cookie?" The "our" would be unnatural, as it is in the prayer.

Matthew follows the words "Our Father" with "who art in heaven," which are not found in Luke. "Our Father who art in heaven" carries the ring of a noble title for God, in much the same way that Duke of Cornwall and Lord of the Isles are used to honor Prince Charles of England on state occasions. But "who art in heaven" adds little meaning to the prayer, because there is never any doubt as to who is being addressed. (It would hardly be our own father on Earth.) And once again there's a loss of natural speech. If a child were to call out "Our Mother who is in the kitchen, thank you for a nice supper," the phrase *who is in the kitchen* can only identify to others where the mother is located. The mother herself hardly needs to be told. "Our Father who art in heaven" projects the same faint effect of telling others where the Father happens to be—in heaven. And that creates a theological puzzle. What exactly does "in heaven" mean? Is heaven the condition of the Father's perfection? Or is it the locus of eternity? What else might it be? "Our Father who art in heaven" raises another question: Is the Father not present in the world around us all the time?

Luke's simple address raises none of these issues. God the Father is everywhere, all the time. He is in heaven in every possible sense, and all around us as well. He does not demand any grand titles, because this is a one-to-one conversation, in private, at bedtime perhaps. And the simplicity of "Father" gives the prayer much greater power than Matthew's grander opening. "Father" rings with the splendor of a natural address to a beloved parent. "Father" can carry solemn respect for parental authority, as in the famous address: "Father, I cannot lie to you. It was I who cut down the cherry tree." It can be touching in its emotional warmth, as in "Father, I'm so sorry," or "Father, I love you." Or it can be a cry of recognition after a long absence. "Oh, Father! I'm back!" This range of emotions is lost in Matthew's "Our Father" because of its formality.

The weakness of Matthew's next addition, "Thy will be done, On earth as it is in heaven," is that it adds little to the prayer's meaning. What it does is give the person praying a quick idea of what "Thy kingdom" is all about, as the prayer goes on its way at the pace of the congregation's recital. The kingdom, we tell ourselves, is a place where God's will is done. But it is so much more than that, and Matthew's addition adds little extra meaning.

His final addition, "But deliver us from evil" (or from the evil one) at the end of the prayer also generates little useful mileage. This petition is nothing more than a repetition of the one that came before, "And lead us not into temptation." The evil Matthew asks that we be delivered from, can only ever arise when we give in to temptation. All the other evil that may come to us is either due to a bad conscience or bad luck or the work of enemies. And we have already prayed that we be spared from these. "Give us this day our daily bread" covers all our nutritional, medicinal, and clothing needs, while "Forgive us... as we forgive [others]" fends off guilt and revenge and all that kind of thing. The only evil that remains at prayer's end is temptation—the risk that we will alienate ourselves from God the Father. But God has already led us away from that evil, too, in the previous petition, "And lead us not into temptation." So, it is not necessary to say, "But deliver us from evil" with Matthew, except to nicely round off the prayer's otherwise abrupt ending.

Matthew's version may contain more than Jesus's words, and therefore less of his intentions, but it is the prayer that is universally loved today. This relentless accounting of the value of every extra word in Matthew seems a brutal exercise to perform on such a melodious act of devotion. But the added fat detracts from the symmetry of Luke's version, which is so pregnant with insights. Luke's prayer is best recited very slowly, with a pause between each petition for contemplation of what has just been said. Prayed like this, Luke's version gives us much deeper insights into Jesus's intentions. Luke's version is the greater guide to the coming of the kingdom.

Luke's Prayer in Depth

"Great literature is simply language charged with meaning to the utmost possible degree," writes Ezra Pound in *How to Read*.[4] This "charged meaning" includes the character of the protagonists, the drama of their relationships, and the sweet comedy or dark tragedy of the story. Luke's prayer contains all these elements. It lays out the characters of God and humans as the two protagonists, and it delineates the relationship between them, as it is now, and as it will be forever. The "story" is an account of how we approach God and how he responds, and how we all arrive together at a happy ending—the coming of the kingdom.

To find these literary treasures, we must look at Jesus's prayer like a squirrel scrutinizing every aspect of an acorn held in its paws. First of all, this prayer is a signpost to the humility of God. The infinite creator of everything is not an overlord. He does not force us to submit to his great power. He sends us a prayer, and merely encourages us to say it. If he were less than humble, he would force us to intone the prayer, and then bend our knee before him. But God the Father leaves us free to make the most important decision in our lives—our relationship with him. Yet the prayer also reminds us that we can never go to God under our own steam. What we do is beg God to help us go to him, and to love him, because we are helpless before him. "Father, Hallowed be thy name [amongst us], Thy kingdom come." In other words, "Help us to respect and love you. We can do nothing by ourselves." And so we learn a sublime paradox—that God the Father is the supreme power, the ruler even of our hearts, and yet he leaves us free to reject him or not. This prayer reveals God's power and his humility at the same moment.

We can also look at the prayer with a magnifying glass trained on each single petition. We discover that the prayer, as it goes along, forces a dynamic growth in our holiness. First, we recognize God as the Father, the most basic religious act. Then, we hallow his name (which can only be done with reverence), and then we call for God's supremacy as King over the nation of the world, a call that can only be made with passion and spiritual commitment. In the second half of the prayer, God responds to our homage and graciously bends down to us, providing bread, forgiveness, and leadership through our faith. By the end of the prayer, God and humankind are united, at least in so far as our sincerity will permit. And that's how this grain of great literature characterizes the drama of man versus God—as a sad story with a happy ending. Luke's prayer is the greatest of all comedies.

We can learn even more about God and his blessings by dissecting the prayer into its six petitions (three in each half) and then rearranging them by lining up each first-half petition with its corresponding second-half petition.

Here's the result:

Before the midpoint:	After the midpoint:
1. Father	1. Give us this day our daily bread
2. Hallowed be thy name	2. And forgive us our sins; we too forgive all those who trespass against us
3. Thy kingdom come	3. And lead us not into temptation

"Father" is found to be the partner of "Give us this day our daily bread." This tells us that God the Father is a parent who provides his children with bread, day by day. The two second-place petitions, "Hallowed be thy name" and "Forgive us our sins" are both prayers for harmony between God and his people. The first prays that God's children will turn away from all their destructive obsessions and honor God the Father's name. If this were ever to be accomplished, God and humankind would soon be united. How long can a Father remain aloof when his children hold his name holy in their hearts? The second petition is also a prayer for reconciliation. God the Father, whose name is now held sacred, reaches down and dispenses forgiveness for all the offenses we have committed against him and others. When this forgiveness has been granted, reconciliation between God and humankind is complete.

Finally, "Thy kingdom come" is partner to "And lead us not into temptation." This is the role of a king, to deliver royal leadership that binds the nation together in harmony and high purpose. In Jesus's prayer, it is the divine King of "Thy kingdom come" who will lead us through the dismal forests and bogs of temptation. That's how we find our way into the kingdom along with the King. This telling symmetry of the three petitions on each side of the midpoint is lost in Matthew's version, because he adds a fourth unnecessary petition to each half.

The Kingdom of the Three-in-One

This examination of the Prayer's petitions, two by two, tells us that God is not monolithic. He is indeed One, but he is also Three-in-One. First, the prayer tells us quite clearly that God is described at least as two Persons, the Father and the King, because we say "Father, Thy kingdom come." But God is also *someone else* who is half concealed. He is the reconciler, as revealed in "Hallowed be thy name" and "Forgive us our sins," which both reconcile us with God. Reconciliation is the job of a priest—to bring God to the people and to take the people to God. Clearly, the two petitions of reconciliation represent this work of a priest.

We are not the priest. We take no action by ourselves to bring about reconciliation. We say "Hallowed be thy name," which means "Please make your name holy amongst us." It is God who will make his name "hallowed" in the community of the world, not us. It is God himself, acting with us and through us, who brings reconciliation between ourselves and the God we have offended. The priest who intercedes on our behalf with God is God himself, the High Priest.

The prayer clearly gives us three portraits of God. He is the Father who creates us and provides bread. He is the High Priest who reconciles us with God the Father when we ask for forgiveness. And he is the King who embraces the people of the world within his mystical rule, when they choose him. Can this be three hats that fit the same head? No! A single person cannot play all these roles.

A father can never be a king to his children, either. He must certainly enforce the rules to build the children's character, but his solemn duty is to relinquish control as the children grow up and develop their own values. A king receives the father's children—now adults—and binds them into the royal nation for the rest of their lives. A king can never allow his subjects to become independent in the way that a father must. If the king's subjects assert their own authority, independent of the king, they commit the foulest of political crimes—treason. Father and king are two incompatible roles. If a father insists on ruling his children like a king when they become adults, he will cripple them. As the children grow up, a father must grow, too—into a wise old friend. The children's homage must be directed to somebody else—the king. The father and the king are two different people.

A father cannot be a priest to his children, either. If the father is wounded by the child, he may extend forgiveness. But if the child remains rebellious, the father can never play the role of reconciler between himself and the child. "Johnny, I want you to persuade me to forgive you, so then I will," doesn't work. Somebody else must direct the child onto the path of reconciliation. This third person, who brings father and child together, is a "priest."

We the children of God the Father are obdurate in our sinfulness. We make resolutions to reform and break them. Or we place a limit on how far we will go in leading "the good life." We are all sinners, all the time. The prayer reminds us of that dismal fact because it makes us ask for forgiveness every time we say it. There is no Level Two version of the prayer for people who have gained forgiveness, and have graduated to spiritual purity. Clearly, we need a priest to reconcile us with the God we offend so often and so easily. And that priest is not God the Father, nor is it God the King. It is God the High Priest. So, Jesus's prayer reveals a God of three persons: the Father who creates us and provides bread; the High Priest who helps us hallow God's name and brings forgiveness; and the King who rules the coming kingdom, in which the rebellious conquer their temptations and love the king and one another.

God is Three-in-One—in other words, the Trinity. This is an ancient understanding that the Christian church also gleaned from other parts of Jesus's teaching. This doctrine of the Trinity was nailed down at the first General Council of Nicaea in 325 A.D. in response to the now forgotten heresy of Arius. But even in the fourth century, the concept of the Three-in-One was well established. Belief in the Holy Trinity goes back to the second and third centuries, according to John Henry Cardinal Newman. He writes in *Tracts Theological and Ecclesiastical,* "Some doctrine or other of a Trinity lies at the very root of the Christian conception of the Supreme Being.... It is impossible to view historical Christianity apart from the doctrine of a Trinity."[5]

The Three-in-One is a mystery that we try to illustrate with many ordinary things. Three raindrops run down a window pane and merge into one big drop, which is then "three drops in one"—supposedly a trinity. But the big raindrop is not really like the Trinity at all, because the three raindrops have all become a single raindrop and lost their identity. The Trinity is not like a shamrock leaf (another popular idea), because the three lobes of the shamrock leaf are separate. They are not three leaves within one single leaf. In the science of mathematics, if three (for the three persons) is divided into one (for the one God), the result is $0.33333\ldots$, with the threes continuing to infinity, where God is thought to reside. But this equation is little more than a curiosity.

The great theologian Thomas Aquinas, and others, developed a penetrating understanding of the Trinity from the opening of John's Gospel: "In the beginning was the Word, and the Word was with God, and the Word was God" (John 1:1). God the Father is perfect, Aquinas said. He must therefore have a perfect knowledge of his own perfection. And that perfect knowledge, or that "Word" as John calls it, is the Son of God, who appeared on Earth as the divine Jesus. (The mystery, of course, is how God's "knowledge" of himself becomes another living person.) These two persons—Father and Son—must love one another, because they know one another's perfection. The love of each for the other is the person of the Holy Spirit. The Son and the Holy Spirit arise from the Father, but the three persons are equal in their divinity, because they are not governed by time or space or limitation. All three persons exist equally from eternity. This vision of the Trinity is compatible with the depiction of the Three-in-One in Jesus's prayer.

In the prayer, the three persons of the Godhead are put forward in the same order in which they came to us on earth. God the Father is revealed first to the ancient Hebrews, through centuries of reflection and the tireless work of the prophets. God the Son, in the person of Jesus, comes down to Earth for thirty years to act as the High Priest through his sacrifice on the cross. And after Jesus's death, the Holy Spirit leads the Apostles and the church toward the coming of the kingdom. This sequence demonstrates how God has gradually revealed his inner glory to us, first as the Father and then as the Son and the King, both in historical reality on Earth and in the prayer.

The prayer tells us, just as Aquinas does, that God the Father has precedence within the Trinity because the Father is the first person we address. In fact, the entire prayer is directed to the Father. "Father," "Thy kingdom come," "Give us bread," "Forgive us," "Lead us." But at another level, we speak to the Father, then to the High Priest, and then to the King, under this overarching shadow of the Father. This confirms the ancient Trinitarian belief in the precedence of God the Father over God the High Priest and God the King. And this precedence offers us another insight into God's great humility. Earthly kings like their power to be honored first, often in fear and trembling, and then they like to be eulogized as loving fathers of their people. An acceptable address to an earthly monarch might be, "Oh mighty King, we revere your very name, Thou art a Father to us all." In Jesus's prayer, God is the Father first—the fountainhead of love. Only then is he recognized as God the King. "Father..., Thy kingdom come." God's role as our loving Father is more important to him than his great power and his right to command our homage as the King.

The three persons are always one God, the prayer insists. The whole incantation: "Father... Thy kingdom come... Forgive us our trespasses" is seamless. You cannot worship the Father without worshiping the High Priest and the King.

The divine Trinity is the living unity of the three persons in one God, which can be illustrated with raindrops and shamrocks and mathematics, but can never be properly defined. It is a mystery beyond our ken. And that is why it is so exhilarating. There is a life in this divine mystery that lifts our spirits from the mundane confinement of things. There is a secret here that frees us from the dreary panoply of science and all its limits and distinctions, where a peach is a peach and an eagle is an eagle, and all material things are separate, each from the other. The incandescent mystery of the Three-in-One reflects the joy of God's glorious freedom from all limitations, which is well beyond our understanding. In seeking the coming of the kingdom with the Father through this prayer, we, too, throw off some of our limitations and become free, a little like God.

The Genders of the Three-in-One

Is the Creator male or female, both, or neither? This may seem an absurd question, considering that gender is merely associated with animal reproduction. But this question must be answered, as we search for the kingdom together, hand in hand, male and female. Jesus's prayer tells us that God is the "King" and the "Father," which declares the deity has more in common with males than with females—or so it seems. A closer look reveals that the divine gender is not that clear. Jesus's prayer is like a hologram, one of those iridescent pictures found on paper currency that reveals a different scene when viewed from various angles. If we look at the prayer the way a robin looks at a worm, with head cocked first on one side, then on the other, the prayer can be seen to depict God as Father, Mother, King, perhaps also as Queen, and certainly as High Priest, of either gender or none.

The key to this shifting vision lies in a contrast between the two halves of the prayer. In the first half, God is described as a father and as a king. There is no ambiguity and no supporting context by which we can modify this masculine assertion. And these two "God is male" petitions stand on either side of "Hallowed be thy name," which can also be considered an address to the "male" deity. God the High Priest—the one who performs the duty of reconciliation with the Father by hallowing his name—also appears to be male like the Father and the King.

The second half of the prayer offers subtle hints that God is also female, as if to allude to divine depths that are not fathomable. The first step toward this intuition is to realize that the person saying the second half of the prayer is a small child. This child must ask God for "bread" every day, which means he or she cannot obtain food without God's help. Second, there is no "please" or "thank you" when the "bread" is asked for and received. It's just a bald "Give us this day our daily bread." A child does not know how to say "please," nor is it expected to do so, because the child has an absolute right to a parent's care. "Please" only becomes a courtesy toward the parent later, as the child grows up. Third, there is a hint of a child's baldly stated Christmas wish list in the use of the word "and" in this part of the prayer. "I've been very good and I want a fire engine and a puppy and a water pistol and a frisbee." Jesus's prayer projects this same childishness: "Give us...bread, *And* forgive us our trespasses, *(And)* we forgive others, *And* lead us not into temptation." This delicate second-half effect is heightened by the absence of "and" in the first half of the prayer, which talks about adults addressing the king.

If the person praying is a small child, then the person he or she talks to is often Mother, not Father. This conclusion rests on the ancient concept of the traditional family, which the prayer invokes from beginning to end. The author, Jesus, depicts God as the "Father" in the opening because God is not only a loving parent, he also exercises authority over the children in the way a male parent does in the traditional family. If Jesus can invoke this traditional family concept through the title "Father," we can employ it in any reflection on the second half of the prayer.

The "small child" saying the prayer is asking for "bread" from its mother. In the traditional family, it is the mother who stays at home and looks after the child. It is the mother who feeds the child "bread" and a hot meal. The father certainly does not serve the children's meals, as we ask this parent to do in "Give us this day our daily bread." Traditional fathers might consider that "women's work." The father earns the income with which to purchase the flour that the mother uses to make the bread. It is also the mother that forgives the small child in the next petition, "And forgive us our trespasses." The father lays down fair rules of conduct for the family and applies them with justice and mercy. It is the mother who shields the child from the father's rightful anger. "We'll clean up this mess before your father comes home. But don't do it again, or I will definitely tell him. Then you'll be in trouble!" How many times has every child heard that from its mother?

The mother may even pay for the child's transgressions out of her own pocket. In the real event of the crucifixion, Jesus pays for the sins of God the Father's children with his own life, just as a mother might do. The Father's laws were already more than fair, but Jesus bends them like rubber in the children's favor. The children are forgiven again and again, and not punished, until the divine judicial system becomes a laughingstock to anybody who thinks they understand the principles of justice. Execute the criminals, some would say. Don't forgive them!

Now, Jesus's magnificent sacrifice is unearned by us. It is partisan in our favor, and shields us from the rightful wrath of God the Father in the way a mother would shield her children. This idea of the male Jesus being a mother is not new. In the thirteenth century, Julian of Norwich, a female English mystic, talked about "Our Mother Christ."[6] In 1984, a statue of Jesus with breasts was presented to a New York museum and raised an outcry of protest from conservative Christians. But the idea persists. The High Priest in Jesus's prayer, the one who reconciles us with the Godhead, is both a man and our dear mother at the same time.

The allusion to God as Mother in Jesus's prayer is always subtle, perhaps because an open declaration that God is both our Mother and our Father at the same time (and a lot more besides) would be information overload for most people. This is a prayer, not a treatise on the mysteries of the Godhead. But the subtlety of the mother-father gender play gives the prayer a living depth that becomes an invitation to deeper reflection. If we say the prayer frequently, and think hard about it, these subtleties become apparent, and we gain a greater appreciation of our relationship with the God to whom we frequently speak.

The allusion to God as Mother continues to the end of the prayer with "And lead us not into temptation." Who walks with a small child, leading it by the hand and keeping it away from the temptation to touch sharp objects and pat dogs that bite? It is more often the mother than the father. At least, that's the conventional view of family that the prayer invokes (not to insist on conventional values, but to provide a framework of reference for our complex relationship with God).

Jesus's prayer reveals all these snapshots of the Godhead's "gender," but they line up into a single vision. The Father creates the bread we eat, but "serves it" lovingly in the way a mother might: "Give us this day our daily bread." The High Priest is male and female at the same time, or neither, in the light of the prayer's neutral language of reconciliation. And at the end of the prayer, God, the divine mother, leads the children through temptation, but it is the male monarch of "Thy kingdom come" (the same person) who leads the spiritual adults into the kingdom of joy. The ruler of a kingdom is just as likely to be a queen as a king—so we might say once in a while that God can be viewed as the Queen and our beloved Mother, if the conservatives will permit it.

God is not a being of great size. He is infinite because he contains no energy, occupies no space, and stands beyond time. This mysterious being stands above and beyond everything that is finite and created. Clearly, then, God is not male or female, because these are notions that arise from the biology of reproduction. Why then does Jesus's prayer allude to God's roles in our lives as Father, Mother, Priest, Priestess, King, and perhaps Queen? In order to tell us one simple fact—that God loves his children in all the ways that a parent possibly can.

The Three-in-One Reflects Our Human Nature

Jesus's prayer also reveals the three dimensions of the human condition. The prayer tells us we are all small children in the eyes of God, we are all spiritual criminals before him, and we are all adults—all at the same time. Clearly, we are children who need a father. And we have a Father, whom we often ignore or forget, the prayer tells us. We are also sinners who need to be reconciled with this Father. And sinning is a lifelong human condition that we never shake off. We have to ask for forgiveness every time we say the prayer. "Forgive us…Forgive us…Forgive us." But the prayer also allows us to call for the coming of God's kingdom after we have been forgiven. In that respect we are adults, because only adults can give homage to a king. Little children will not bow before a king unless told to do so. "Who's that man with a crown on his head, Daddy?" "Shush, that's the king." "What's a king, Daddy?" In welcoming the king through "Thy kingdom come," we grow up from children who look for and find their father into spiritual adults who are ready to take full responsibility for their actions and seek the king's nation on Earth.

Little children, sinners, adults—these three contemporaneous conditions of our humanity are woven through the prayer in many subtle ways that illustrate the complexity of our spiritual nature. For instance, the child's demand, "Father, give us bread" is balanced by the whole prayer's honorific structure, which is consistent with an address to royalty by a loyal adult subject. "Oh Mighty One! You are a true father to your people [Father]. May your greatness be known all over the world [Hallowed be thy name], and may your kingdom flourish without challenge [Thy kingdom come]." This is high homage that could have been given safely to the ancient pharaohs or the kings of Persia. At the same time, it is a child asking his Father for the bread that is his right.

There are other paradoxes of infancy and adulthood in this prayer. The little child saying the prayer is not just naughty; he commits heinous crimes against his Father, such as murder and rape. The guilty child calls out "Father" and is forgiven, and starts to grow into a spiritual adult, born again into the coming of the kingdom with the innocence of a child. "At that time, the disciples came to Jesus and asked, 'Who is the greatest in the kingdom of heaven?' He called a child, whom he put among them, and said, 'Truly I tell you, unless you change and become like children, you will never enter the kingdom of heaven. Whoever becomes humble like this child is the greatest in the kingdom of heaven'" (Matthew 18:1-4). We must become spiritual adults in front of the King before we can understand how to be as innocent as children.

As we repeat this living prayer with devotion, we change from a sinner grown old in the obscenities, to a little child who has found his Father, to an enlightened adult who has the humility of a child. But we are always all three at the same time, a condition that is mystically woven throughout our spirituality.

Jesus's Prayer As Mythic Journey

Jesus's prayer has been translated into almost all the languages on earth. In Quenya, J. R. R. Tolkien's invented language of the elves, it reads as "Á taremma I ëa han ëa, na aire esselya" (Our Father who art in heaven, hallowed be thy name). It has been rendered into Klingon, the guttural language created by an American linguistics professor for a war-loving race of aliens in the science fiction television series *Star Trek*. It has been translated into Maltese and Norwegian, Chinese and Urdu, Japanese and Swahili. The devout efforts of hundreds of translators are proof that Jesus's prayer is more than a list of the ways God loves us, or a peep at the mysteries of the Trinity.

It is part of the spiritual life of most Christian people. It also carries the ring of myth—an ancient tale that resonates deep in our consciousness. Before Christopher Columbus began his journey of discovery to America, he reputedly met a dying captain on a ruined vessel that drifted into a nearby port. The mariner told him that a new land existed far over the horizon. This dying mariner's tale is supposedly what motivated Columbus to make his historic journey. But the story has no factual basis, says author Miles Harvey in *The Island of Lost Maps*.[7] It is only a myth that personifies the action of destiny in Columbus's journey. And this myth fits a common pattern. "A hero starts his journey in many myths with the blessing of a protective figure (often an . . . old man)," says Joseph Campbell in his study of legends, *The Hero with a Thousand Faces*. "What such a figure represents is the benign protecting power of destiny. The fantasy [of a protective figure] is a reassurance—a promise that the peace of Paradise, which was known first within the mother womb, is not to be lost."[8] Other ancient legends talk of a long, arduous journey that reaches a final destination where there is only peace and happiness, such as Shangri La.

Jesus's prayer fits all these myths. It is a hero's journey of the spirit, presided over by a protective figure as old as time: God the Father. And it tells of reaching a land of perfect happiness—the kingdom of God. This prayer is nothing less than the greatest adventure of humankind—abandonment of the false safety within the fortress of the ego in favor of a perilous journey to a holy and beautiful homeland.

The traveler sets out by throwing away his most desired possession, the right to feel superior (or God-like) toward others. He says "Father" and admits his place is not at the top of the heap, where he thought he belonged. The Father is at the top, and the person praying admits he can no longer play God in the lives of others.

This first step is one of the most daring acts a person can ever take. Instead of the dreary, never-ending struggle for a sense of superiority, the spiritual adventurer calls on God the Father to direct his life toward an open, loving encounter with God the Father's other children. Openness to others is always fraught with the risk of rebuff or contempt or even treachery by the persons to whom we lay ourselves open. The adventurer embraces these hazards because he or she is not alone. As in so many myths, the traveler is accompanied by a protective figure, God the Father, who promises that "the peace of Paradise is not to be lost."

This first prayer to God the Father acts as powerful therapy, freeing the speaker from all the destructive cravings of pride, anxiety, and greed, so that he or she may be ready for the deeper spiritual journey. Most of these inward obsessions come from the same source—anxiety. Wealth and honor, the products of greed and pride, do provide comfort, but it is superficial security. Deeper down, the anxiety that accompanies all these destructive impulses remains, and is often founded on fear of annihilation. The worriers are afraid they may cease to exist as the people they know themselves to be—perhaps an accountant with a loving wife and two cars in the garage—all of which is threatened by a real or imagined financial calamity. When anxiety is severe, it can become an irrational fear that the troubled person will cease to exist at all, because he or she does not have the power to defend his or her own existence against the heavy misfortune that is supposedly looming. This spiritual terror is not fear of death. It is an irrational fear that we are not strong enough to defend our own existence and will simply cease to be, although it is never articulated as such. Shakespeare's "To be or not to be?" captures this dread and hints at more than Hamlet's uncertainty over whether to live or not live. An apprehension of indefinable peril often lies within the very state of being human.

To say "Father" is to throw away all this miasmic fear of misfortune. To say "Father" is to walk the high, mountain trails of the spirit without fear of falling over the precipices close by. The adventurer comes to understand that his existence is not balancing on a knife edge after all. It is an unconditional gift from God the Father, which is unaffected by any action of the adventurer's. This is not fatalism. It is its opposite: faith. To say "Father" is to banish anxiety, even in times of famine or war.

The pilgrim continues on his exhilarating journey—word by word, step by step—through the prayer, and through his life. In "Thy kingdom come," the adventurer's gaze is turned even farther away from his self-inflicted, gut-wrenching agonies toward the exhilarating goal of building an embrace between this loving God the Father and the whole community. "Give us this day our daily bread" abandons all care about physical needs. If the adventurer is wealthy, he abandons greed and turns his attention to spiritual matters. If he is poor, he trusts he will receive enough "bread" by the grace of God to stay alive as he goes about his Father's other business—fearlessly. The adventurer, rich or poor, comes to rely on God to provide just enough food each day as he prays for it. This is the essence of all adventure, treading fearlessly into places where we are not sure we will live or die.

The final petition, "And lead us not into temptation," brings spiritual security, because where there is forgiveness and no fear of temptation there can be no guilt, nor any fear of guilt, only the blessed relief of a clean happiness.

Once we leave the safe house of the self with all its ugly furniture and embark on Jesus's prayer, God the Father takes us hand in hand on a walk into the paradise of the coming of the kingdom to meet the King, who is himself. Along that road, we learn to act in a concrete way in the community's favor as it stands in the love of God. Praying for bread for the community is worthless without sharing our own bread. Asking for forgiveness without forgiving others is an injustice that will bear no fruit. Jesus's prayer must be lived wholeheartedly, not just spoken. And living a good life is always an adventure.

As the journey continues, the pilgrim moves closer to the coming of the kingdom—the ultimate goal of all adventurers, whether they be mountain climbers or saints. The spiritual traveler establishes a deeper friendship with God. He is also awakened to the real world around him through the three great paradoxes of Christianity. He enjoys a greater fullness of humanity by the abandonment of advantage. He experiences a more intense enjoyment of worldly pleasures by means of a lesser attachment to them. And he gains a realization, as St. Francis of Assisi put it, of "our worthlessness," which is empowered by the infinite love of God.

"Religion . . . is the greatest and healthiest exercise the human mind can have," said Swami Vivekananda, a twentieth-century Hindu sage. "This struggle to grasp the Infinite . . . is the grandest and most glorious that man can make."[9] Vivekananda may well have been talking about Jesus's prayer for the coming of the kingdom. It is not recited once, or twice, or two hundred times. It is living flesh of the spirit, and can be spoken time and time again to progressively enrich the person praying. This handful of words is an endless resource of true understanding, healing, and spirituality.

2

Father

God the Father is the origin of all human beings. He exists within and around everything in the universe. The universe is sustained by his will and if he were ever to stop willing it, everything would vanish. To try to understand this first person of the Trinity is to try to pierce a diamond with a wooden drill. That's why Jesus calls him Father—not to capture his real essence, which is ineffable, but to give us some appreciation of where he stands in relation to us and to the universe. The Father is the one who creates and the one who cares deeply about his creation.

We are asked to return the Father's love for his happiness and our own happiness, and out of simple justice. We begin to perform this delightful duty by calling out "Father." As we do so, we start conversations clicking over within the soul. Each conversion occurs at a deeper level and further enhances the maturity of the person praying. Gradually, saying "Father" leads us to an ever closer reliance on the love of God all the time. This one-word entreaty also engineers a cataclysmic change in our attitude toward the people around us, whom we now recognize as sacred brothers and sisters to be loved and cherished. In holy people, such as Francis of Assisi, the love of the Creator generates a unity with birds and animals that is barely comprehensible to the rest of us. Learning to love God the Father is a source of many wonders emanating from him and from his creation.

"Father" is a statement of fact, an admission of the reality of all human life at every moment. We recognize that the being who created light, water, and sky is the parent of the human race, now and forever. But "Father" is also a broader confession. It acknowledges the same relationship between the Creator and every individual that ever lived, regardless of whether he or she worships or hates God. Any person, good or bad, can say "Father" and receive the benefits of this universal truth. This relationship of Father and child is unalterable by any action we or God will ever take. The word *Father* opens the tight-fisted heart and confesses the beautiful, life-giving bond between God and this man or this woman, as well as with all humanity.

We think we are alone as we try to conquer our base urges and struggle to overcome the hardships that infest our lives. By turns, we are triumphant, content, worried, and angry. We are always mourning loved ones—the living we alienate by our disgraceful conduct or the dead who are gone forever. We regret the loss of a promotion or the decline of the stock market. We fret over our own nastiness, recalling it with pain, even after the victims have forgotten. "The trilling wire in the blood sings below inveterate scars, appeasing long forgotten wars,"[1] as T. S. Eliot put it. Our sorrows are not all in our minds. Some of us bear crushing injustice, such as those who are jailed for years for crimes they did not commit and are punished in the penal system for not admitting their guilt. These cruel misfortunes are compounded by crimes we do happily commit. Sexism and homophobia corrode our best values. People of one ethnic origin deny advancement to people of another, and there is never a satisfying explanation. We all have to make our way against these violent currents of life. This is the basic condition of humankind throughout the ages.

To say "Father" is to confess that we are never alone in this foot-sucking quagmire of filth. We realize with an immense sigh of relief that we do not have to solve all our problems by ourselves. The solution is in the hands of the all-powerful Creator, who loves us and because of this love, will not abandon us. Every person who says "Father" reaches this understanding, even when he says it for the first time. This joyful discovery of an all-caring parent brings peace of mind greater than any other.

Does God the Father Really Love Us?

"Why did God make us?" the old Catholic catechism demands to know. The answer it trumpets is this: "God made us to know him, to love him, and to serve him." This admonition is taken further by *The Question and Answer Catholic Catechism* written in recent years by John A. Hardon, a Jesuit priest. "God wants us to know him because he is the Eternal Truth, to love him because he is our most loveable God, and to serve him because he is the Sovereign Lord."[2] This lofty view of the divine was developed at a time when Christians looked up to the kings who ruled them, supposedly with divine authority. God was viewed as a giant mirror of these magnificent people. It is always tempting to understand God's authority in the light of human values and experience.

This vision of God the Father is not in keeping with what Jesus teaches us. Are we to believe that God is so proud of being "the Eternal Truth" that he creates people to know this truth—and buttress his pride? Did God the Father really create human beings because he wanted "servants"? If this were true, God would appear to be self-centered. The truth is much more startling, and most humbling. God the Father made us so that he might love us and serve us. Having done that, he hopes we will love him in return. But God the Father will still love us no matter how we respond. And tragically, he knows he created some of us in vain.

If God the Father loves us, why are our lives so full of suffering, and why must they end in the horror of death? Why hasn't this divine Father arranged his affairs so that we can live in bliss with him forever? Isn't that what a caring parent would do? This enigma is one of the great mysteries of the human condition. It has puzzled philosophers, pharmacists, bakers, and bums throughout the ages. The easy answer is that God the Father is not a sentimental parent who shields his children from risk. He knows that tough love, with its content of pain, is more effective in helping his children grow up than pandering to them would ever be. But this answer is not satisfactory. Why do suffering and death seem so antagonistic to human well-being, if they come from God the Father?

The Garden of Eden

The Biblical authority on the origin of hardship and death is the tale of the Garden of Eden and the rebellious conduct of our "first parents" that led to their doom. This story holds many riches, but not those commonly taken from it. "And the Lord God planted a garden in Eden, in the east; and there he put the man whom he had formed. Out of the ground, the Lord God made to grow every tree that is pleasant to the sight and good for food"

(Genesis 2:8-9). God creates Eve from Adam's rib to be his companion. The two protohumans enjoy free food and the perfect climate—they don't need clothes. And there's little work to do. Adam tills the soil around the fruit trees. Eve is his "helper and partner." The pair are going to live forever because death has not been invented. But they blow it all by sinning and get thrown out of the garden to work and die outside. That's the story in a nutshell, but we have to ask three questions. Who are Adam and Eve? What are suffering and death really all about? And what does this story tell us?

The Australian aborigines talk about the creation of the world as "the dream time," a period of divine imagination that gave birth to all we know. The Adam and Eve tale has the same dreamlike quality. Eden is far away "in the east." It is a fantastical garden, in which the all-powerful God walks among the trees like a human, without noticing what the others are up to. There is a walking, talking serpent who beguiles the woman, and then loses its voice and legs as a punishment and becomes what we know as a snake. And finally there is a nightmare of shame and exile, after which Adam and Eve wake up in the real world. The nightmare lingers, even for us.

Why is this story told in dream time? Because long ago, dreams were thought to be the way God inspired us. Jesus's father, Joseph, has a dream in which he learns the pregnant Mary is not a fallen woman, and he marries her. They flee to Egypt after Joseph has a second dream warning him not to stay in Judea. In Genesis, the writer cast the story of Eden in dream form because he wanted us to know it as a divinely inspired insight into something we can never discover for ourselves—the creation. All cultures have similar stories.

The Garden of Eden is not the stuff of the real world. Adam and Eve have nothing to accomplish for their personal growth. There are no children and no relatives. There is none of the spice of danger that comes with adventure. There is no meat to eat, because there is no death. There is none of the fun of wearing hats. There is no Chinese food, no sea to bathe in. Living naked in an orchard, Adam and Eve have only three activities to while away their days: gossiping, games, and gardening. This Eden is but a dream of what the ancient Jews ached for most—rest from the hard work of making a living with stone age tools, and respite from the death of loved ones in a harsh land. Eden is like all paradises embedded in the subconscious of ancient peoples. It reflects the harsh realities of the readers' lives, in reverse, in the currency of dreams. In desert traditions, paradise is a place for men, with fountains dispensing what the land does not offer freely—

water. Dates are abundant everywhere, along with the seventy-seven "perpetual virgins" assigned to each man (a dream of perfect sex). For the native people of North America, paradise is a "happy hunting ground," where the food is meat, not fruit. Every arrow brings down a meal, and the people never go hungry. What these paradises represent are the perfervid dreams of the poor. No paradise ever portrays the real joy of God's kingdom, because that is unknowable.

In the garden, God imposes one restriction on Adam and Eve—do not eat the fruit from the tree that brings knowledge of good and evil, that one "over there." Adam and Eve are not told "You mustn't eat bananas, or mangoes." They are forbidden the fruit that will open their eyes to "the real world." They are told not to commit sin—any sin—because if they do, they will taste the fruit of sin (evil) as well as the fruit of good, which they already enjoy.

The first couple eats the "forbidden fruit." And into this one act, the author of Genesis cleverly conflates almost all human offenses. Adam and Eve hoist upon themselves a blasphemous pride by deciding they know better than God. Their decision is an abuse of God's trust, because he is "looking the other way" when they commit the offense. Adam and Eve are thieves, because the forbidden fruit is not theirs to pick. They commit the sin of greed, because they already have other gastronomic delights. And sexual perversion is hinted at in the penile form of Eve's serpent tempter. What the ancient writer has constructed so brilliantly is a story that captures the essence of spiritual rebellion at all times. Sin is the arrogance to attribute to one's self the divine rights that belong to God. It is a refusal to accept God's blessings as being enough for our happiness. It is a decision to take what we want, regardless of the consequences. The universality of Adam and Eve's sin is one clue to what the writer is trying to tell us.

The penalty for Adam and Eve's sin is toil, suffering, and death. "Cursed is the ground because of you," God tells Adam, "in toil you shall eat of it all the days of your life; thorns and thistles it shall bring forth for you, and you shall eat the plants of the field. By the sweat of your face you shall eat bread until you return to the ground, for out of it you were taken; you are dust, and to dust you shall return" (Genesis 3:17-19). Eve is promised pain in childbirth and submission to the rule of her husband. Life outside the garden begins with a curse, one that hangs over all of us today after Adam and Eve's nightmare.

As we study the story, it becomes clear that it is not as simple as it seems. It sparkles with subtle truths and intriguing contradictions. While Adam and Eve are in their innocent state, for instance, they are told they must not eat the forbidden fruit, "for in the day that you eat of it, you shall die" (Genesis 2:17). After their sinful feast, God expels them from the garden saying, "See, the man has become like one of us, knowing good and evil; and now, he might reach out his hand and take also from the tree of life, and eat, and live forever" (Genesis 3:22). The fruit of one tree brings death to the innocent; the fruit of another brings eternal life to the sinful. What are we to make of that? And who is the "us" that God refers to?

First of all, the writer is exploring the same mystery we find in Jesus's prayer—how can we be three things all at once: God's children, criminals, and adults. In the tale, Adam and Eve are the children of God, who made them and cared for them. They become criminals, as we do, by their own choosing. And by sinning, they give up the rights of beloved children and become adults who must shoulder responsibility for their actions. The ancient writer also identifies what makes humans different from animals, and from angels. Humans have a knowledge of good and evil that raises us high above the teeming jungle floor, and yet we suffer and die, unlike the eternal angels. The writer of Genesis was clearly a person of great wisdom, whose spirituality engaged his attention more than his animal nature did. So he saw human beings as spiritual creatures first, and then made them travel in the wrong direction. We gained our knowledge of evil, he says, by falling from an angelic state. And it's this fall that allegedly subjected us to the death suffered by the animals below us. The theory of evolution—written so long after Genesis—tells us, instead, that we evolved from the animals and acquired a godlike knowledge of good and evil as a precious divine gift. The author of Genesis could not have anticipated this theory.

But the author does point to the key place of human death in the joyous generation of life. Adam and Eve are called husband and wife, but they did not make love in the garden, at least, so it seems. Idling among the fruit trees, they are innocent about their nakedness because the "shame" a person feels about exposing his or her genitals is related to the privacy of the sex act. Sex is not happening in the garden, because there is no need for birth to replace the undying. After they sin, Adam and Eve "discover" their nakedness, and "cover their shame" with fig leaves. After this sexual awakening, they are expelled from the garden. The story then reports, for the first time, that Adam "knew" his wife. She gives birth to children to replace the now mortal parents. And this "first woman" finally gets a name—Eve, which means "the mother of mankind." This reading allows us to turn death from a curse into a boon. If Adam and Eve's sin led to death, it also led to the blessing of life for every one of us, because if Adam and Eve had not sinned, they would never have left the Garden and borne descendants. Adam and Eve's sin is the source not only of death, but also of the gift of life, and within life, the joy of sexual love. At least that is the implication of the story.

But what of the story's insistence that suffering is an accursed consequence of sin? That's a harder one to tease out. In Stone Age cultures human suffering was indeed considered a divine punishment for bad deeds—perhaps an individual's sins or his father's or his grandfather's. And so, the cascading of Adam and Eve's curse through the generations would have rung true for Stone Age people as they listened to the story around a campfire. "Ah! That's why life is so hard. We are all the children of those sinners Adam and Eve." This Stone Age spin on sin still has legs, even today. *Apologetics and Catholic Doctrine* published in 1953 teaches that "God gave Adam sanctifying grace and immunity from death.... By his sin he lost these precious gifts... and transmitted to [us] his guilt and its evil consequences." The author, the late Archbishop M. Sheehan, insists that Adam's story is a literal explanation of the hardship and death in the world. "Original sin... is transmitted to us through... the flesh we have inherited from Adam...."[3]

Sin and death are indeed linked, but it's not a fleshly link, as the Archbishop contends. It's a spiritual link summed up by Paul as "the wages of sin is death" (Romans 6:23). In this light, Adam and Eve can be viewed as the entire human race, which indeed they are, at that time in the story. The garden is an allegory of a true paradise on earth—one in which innocent people enjoy a happiness that is symbolized by an abundance of fruit, which involves no killing. Adam and Eve are also fully open to one another, which is portrayed by their nakedness—a blissful vulnerability to God and to one another, secure as they are in a loving world. We could all live in that Eden today, if we chose to cultivate the innocence that God the Father demanded from Adam and Eve. After their sin, Adam and Eve are ashamed and cover their nakedness with fig leaves, which is the end to their honesty. Like them, we learn the "wages of sin"—the spiritual death of envy, anger, and revenge. In this reading, Eden and the country outside are spiritual territory, not real terrestrial geography.

But the question comes back. Our souls suffer and die through sin, but why do our bodies suffer and die as well? Certainly not as a consequence of sin. Smallpox doesn't flare up after an act of embezzlement, nor does a fatal fall follow a rape. In fact, a car crash can maim a person who is in a state of grace, and a decent person can slip on the ice and die of a broken neck. Many worthy people suffer terribly, and many bad people live in comfort. The Bible itself points out that suffering may be unearned, as in the poignant story of the good man Job.

We have a long way to go to solve this ancient conundrum. We begin our journey with the conviction that the God who inflicted agony and death on us is our loving Father. Jesus tells us this forcefully. So we must reexamine the three "curses" of Adam and Eve—toil, hardship, and death—in the light of this divine love. After careful consideration, we may conclude the opposite of what Genesis says: that in fact, these three "curses" are some of God the Father's greatest gifts. They can be seen as signs of his great mercy rather than his cruelty.

The Father's Gift of Life

If we are to understand agony and death in light of divine love, we must first ask: What is life? Shakespeare's Macbeth gives the nihilistic answer. "Life's but a walking shadow; a poor player, that struts and frets his hour upon the stage, and then is heard no more: it is a tale told by an idiot, full of sound and fury, signifying nothing."[4] Life comes from out of the void, says Macbeth, and creates nothing but noise. All that remains after each life is nourishment for the trees in the cemetery.

But others see life's radiance. "What is life?" asked Crowfoot, the great Native American leader, in 1890. "It is the flash of a firefly in the night. It is a breath of a buffalo in the wintertime. It is as the little shadow that runs across the grass and loses itself in the sunset."[5] Crowfoot saw life as a light in the darkness, which illuminates more than the burning candle. Life is within matter, but not of matter, Crowfoot says. Its essence is its creativity, and that is sharpened by the inevitability of life's end. Death, far from being a curse, is the source of life's brilliance.

The Epistle of James gives the Christian view:

> Come now, you who say, "Today or tomorrow we will go to such and such a town and spend a year there doing business and making money." Yet you do not even know what tomorrow will bring. What is your life? For you area mist that appears for a little while and then vanishes. Instead you ought to say, "If the Lord wishes, we will live and do this or that." James 4:13-15

Life is from God, James says, and belongs to God. To rely on one's life is to fail to understand the fragility of God's gift, which even the animist Crowfoot understood. To rely on life's security is to place more importance on the gift than on the giver, and to value living over life.

The Father makes each life out of "dust." He graciously sustains it every moment, and prevents that life and the whole world from becoming nothing again, through his omnipotent will. In every life, each new moment of time is a brilliant gift from the Father. It is a gift that is unearned, and cannot be expected. That's why the "future" as depicted in science fiction like *Star Trek* and *Babylon V* is only ever that—fiction. What we think of as the future is only a dream of the generosity of the Father, which, like a fairy tale, actually comes true. Moment by moment, the Father wills finite time and space to continue for his beloved children and for all his other mysterious purposes. The Father generously creates in the unfolding present the future we may have dreamed of, though never in the form in which we dreamed it. Each new moment is the dawn of creation, and perhaps that is why so much of the world is so beautiful—it is always fresh.

Life is a free gift, and one that aches to repay itself. This truth was understood by a few Polish lancers at the beginning of World War II. On September 1, 1939, German tanks massed menacingly on the Polish border, ready to race forward to conquer half of Poland while the Soviet Union stole the other half. Terrified Poles fell to their knees and prayed "Our Father, who art in heaven." They could place their faith in God, but not in the Polish army, because it was poorly equipped and unprepared for conflict. Its soldiers had only one solid asset: a reputation for gallantry. And their actions surprised the Poles and the world.

The generals and the men knew they had no hope of defeating the Germans, but they felt passionately that they could not leave their beloved Poland undefended, whatever the cost. That would be dishonorable. The lancers faced the oncoming tanks on horseback on a low rise. The commanders called out "For the Fatherland!" and sabers were unsheathed, a sight that had stricken fear into the hearts of many other, more antique enemies. The horses began to trot, and then they galloped straight toward the approaching tanks. Most of the troopers were cut down by machine-gun fire. The few that reached the tanks stuck their swords into the observation slits, hoping to harm the drivers. The Germans leaned back in their seats and laughed, and the tanks continued their brutal way into the heart of Poland. The few Polish soldiers that survived the attack were rounded up and taken into slavery in German armament factories, where they were brutalized for the rest of the war as a reward for their gallantry.

This legendary Polish cavalry charge definitely happened, many people swear. But others insist it is a myth of the courage of the ill-equipped Polish army as it fought heroically on horseback against German mechanized divisions. Factual or not, this story is true in the very best sense. The devotion of the Polish military during that war gave the Polish people a sense of pride in the next forty-five years of brutal occupation by the Germans and the Russians, a pride they desperately needed to lift their spirits. Polish people knew in their hearts throughout those dark years that they were a people of character and integrity, even of nobility, in part because of this selfless military action. Life is for living, the Polish lancers declared, as they rode to their deaths. Life is not for hoarding.

The arrow of human life is like a beam of light, which science tells us is transmitted as both waves and particles, two incompatible forms of radiation that somehow coexist in light. It is the same with human life. The individual "particles" of life are John Donnelly living in Plymouth, Maria-Loreta Cauchi living in Sliema, and Li Fung in Halifax—all unique persons, materially and spiritually separate from one another. But they are also part of the river of life that passes down in "waves" through ancestors to a grandfather, a mother, a son, and a daughter in an ever-widening flow of being and begetting. This mystical union of the individual and the community is well understood by warriors and saints. They live and die by the knowledge that they are uniquely themselves, and are also a part of the nation of God. At times, they believe, the particle of life must be subsumed into the river of life, through death, which is what the Polish lancers did. And if we look at life as both an indivisible river and as a stream of droplets, we may find some of the answers to the mystery of life and death. But we must look at all the blessings and "curses" that come from God the Father all together, if we are to understand any one of them.

Toil: The First "Curse" of Adam and Eve

What is life? In a strictly material sense, life is the ability to work. Birds work their way across the sky. Wood lice work to masticate rotting wood. Beavers work to build dams. People work at living. And all work boils down to transportation—the movement of a quantity of matter through a stretch of space over a period of time. This is true of muck spreading and bricklaying, walking and swimming. It is even true of thinking, which transports electrical currents and chemicals from one neuron in the brain to another. Life is the action of transporting things, which we call work. Without work, there is no life.

Work may be disagreeable because, at times, we would rather sleep or sunbathe. And long ago, people had too little food to be able to work hard, and too little time to snooze and play. That's why the book of Genesis labels toil as a curse. But this view is simplistic. The pros and cons of work are much more complex. They are even paradoxical and mystical.

Every human being is fenced in by limits, even if they are only the constant need for food and shelter. And there is no such thing as a perfect human being anyway. Each person is handicapped by a weak heart, or a weak knee, or ignorance, or something else. That is why we must make crutches and blackboards, cars and scalpels. But none of us can do all the things other people can do. So one becomes a farmer. Another a teacher. A third a plumber. Our individual limitations are burst open by the work we do collectively. And that's how we stand above the lifeless world—by making food and acetaminophen, by playing tubas, and by printing Bibles. Without work, there would be no material or spiritual life for the individual or for the community. Work is finite in and of itself—it is merely transportation—but it helps overcome our finiteness. Work supports the flash of the infinite within our being.

Work is a paradox. It is a burden, and the very blessing that wards off death. But it's not even that simple. There are divine mysteries at work, within work. The action of good or bad luck gives work's outcome an unexpected character, which can make it more satisfying—or defeat it all together. A top-gun fighter pilot runs into wind shear and his plane crashes out of control. His expertise is incapable of maintaining his elevation. He runs out of luck. Work is also made unpredictable by our rich capacity to err, most of the time. And mistakes take us down highways that we didn't even know existed. Who, for example, discovered that distilling ants produces formic acid? Was that the outcome of a happy error? Mistakes can also defeat our ambitions, until we become utterly disheartened. All in all, our work's mistakes have a mystical quality. They broaden our humanity by making our collective reach greater or less than our grasp, in ways we never expect.

These two jokers in work's pack of cards—error and luck—bring to all human lives a mosaic of success and failure, of insight and bafflement. Between the interstices of these paving stones we make our character flourish and our nobility grow, or fail. Through the gift of work, and the gamble of chance, God the Father has blessed us with an opportunity, one that can take us in unexpected directions, with his own unseen guidance. Work also makes us a little like God himself. We cannot use it to violate the natural law, but we can pit one natural force against another for our own purposes. When we dig soil, we pit muscle against mud, under our direction, not God's. When we drive a car, we pit the laws of combustion against the laws of friction. In these ways, we take the initiative away from God the Father and the nature he created, and become like little gods ourselves. And so, we can use work to sin or to redeem sin, to live or to die. In that sense, work is the divine platform on which the edifice of human dignity is built, or collapses. Work is not a curse, as Genesis would have us believe. In fact, we were all blessed when our "first parents" were given work to do. Work is a divine opportunity to rise up to God the Father in love. Work is the vehicle of our freedom. "A perpetual holiday is a good working definition of Hell," as Bernard Shaw put it.

Suffering: The Second "Curse" of Adam and Eve

Adam and Eve win food with their "toil" from a Middle Eastern soil that is cursed and yields "thorns and thistles," according to Genesis 3. "By the sweat of your face you shall eat bread until you return to the ground," Adam is told. A diet of fruit, which falls ripe from the tree, has been replaced with bread, which requires tilling the ground, sowing the seed, irrigation, harvesting, winnowing, grinding, kneading, and baking. The "toil" promised to Adam means more than labor. It stands for incessant hard work, and implies the suffering that goes with a body worn out by work and the diseases of old age.

The question is why God the Father would fill the lives of his children with such pain and misery. And this is the biggest barrier to spirituality for some people. If they endure suffering themselves, they descend into a contempt for God, who has "singled them out" for punishment. Why me, they keep saying, as they are trundled into the operating room. But why me? Those who see other people's agonies become atheists, arguing that the pain of good people proves there is no loving divinity, if there is any divinity at all. Especially troubling is the Holocaust, one of the most horrific crimes in the history of the world. How can God the Father allow this to happen to anybody, let alone the Jews, the people that brought monotheism to the world and remained loyal to him through thick and thin?

The English author Thomas Hardy thought he knew the answer. In one poem, he refers to God as "The dreaming dark, dumb thing that turns the handle of this idle Show."[6] And this is an optimistic Hardy. In most of his writing, a malevolent fate torments the characters, thwarting their noble ambitions and plunging them into tragedy. God is not detached, Hardy liked to preach. God is filled with animus against all human beings. Some Father! Long ago, G. K. Chesterton dismissed Hardy as "a sort of village atheist brooding and blaspheming over the village idiot."[7] And Hardy's work is no longer widely read. But his theology is far from original. It echoes that of the ancient Greeks, whose myths talked about the gods—Zeus and his pals—toying with humans for play. Another English poet, Lord Alfred Tennyson, depicted the Greek gods' hedonistic apathy in "The Lotos-Eaters." "Careless of mankind... they lie beside their nectar... where they smile in secret, looking over wasted lands, Blight and famine, plague and earthquake, roaring deeps and fiery sands, Clanging fights and flaming towns, and sinking ships and praying hands."[8] The Greeks dreamed up their callous gods to explain the cruel vagaries of nature. But their attribution of indifference to the divine is a shallow reading of the world, in part because it lacks modern insights.

In the animal kingdom, pain brings wonderful spiritual benefits. When a lion clamps its teeth into a water buffalo's hide, the pain forces the buffalo to fight to the death, and that struggle preserves the balance of the two forces at the kill. All predator-prey contests are finely balanced on this knife-edge of pain, and the hunter's possible failure. That's why the predators never eliminate all the prey, and the prey don't all escape the predators. In this deadly contest, predator and prey evolve into faster and stronger beasts. Pain is part of the arsenal of God the Father's creativity, which has given us magically beautiful tigers and gazelles and spiders and dragonflies, all created in prehistoric times through the medium of terror. Pain is part of divine creativity and brings us the grace of natural beauty.

Human beings suffer for many reasons: the attack of bacteria, the bite of scorpions, falling rocks, car accidents, and a thousand other afflictions.

At the very least, the luckiest of us are doomed to old age with all its hardships. Nobody can escape that. But why is there pain in all this? Why doesn't the body deal with disease and decay painlessly? There are scientific insights and spiritual ones.

The scientific view is that pain informs the body it is being harmed, and in the end, ensures a long life. Those few people who never suffer pain harm themselves at night, because they do not feel the discomfort that causes people to roll over in their sleep. Their blood pools in the same position all night and damages their internal organs. Those who never experience fear don't live long lives, either. They take risks that others would shy away from, and endanger themselves unnecessarily. Pain and fear protect us and give us a safe journey into maturity, where we can love God the Father with a fuller heart, or hate him as the author of all these "curses."

Pain also stands as an emblem of our capacity to love. When a person breaks a leg, he is not left to find food as best he can, and perhaps starve, as an animal would. Others feed him, while he endures his pain, until he is well again. People with cancer die slowly, in drawn-out agony, because we care for them. They are not culled quickly from the herd by predators that attack the ailing. By feeding the sick, we prolong human life and express our love, but we also extend pain. In that way, much of our suffering comes about because we have risen above the animals, rather than because we have fallen from Eden. Suffering is the emblem of the divine spark that burns within us, rather than the curse of our sin.

Pain is a divine blessing in another way—as the austere soil on which a person's spirituality can truly grow. In the Old Testament, God allows "the evil one" to kill Job's cattle and children (Job 1:13-19) and afflict him with painful skin diseases (2:7). Job's anguish prompts him and his comforters to speculate intensely about God's methods. Pain "grows them up," as it can do for all people. Soldiers in agony on the battlefield often call out to God for help, even if they were formerly atheists. Spiritually indifferent persons turn to the comfort of prayer when they suffer a sudden misfortune. And perhaps a closeness to God through prayer can actually ease pain.

In 1945, Kim Malthe-Bruun, a 22-year-old Danish cabin boy, suffered and died as a prisoner of the Nazis. He had gallantly opposed the occupation of his country and joined an armed underground organization in Copenhagen. After being captured by the Nazis and tortured in his cell, he wrote these words: "Since then I have often thought of Jesus. I can well understand the measureless love he felt for all men, and especially for those who took part in driving the nails into his hands," according to a letter printed in *Dying We Live*.[9] After receiving the death sentence, Malthe-Bruun wrote passionately to his sweetheart:

> Remember... that every sorrow turns into happiness—but very few people will in retrospect admit this to themselves. They wrap themselves in their sorrow, and habit leads them to believe that it continues to be sorrow, and they go on wrapping themselves up in it. The truth is that after sorrow comes a maturation, and after maturation comes fruit.[10]

This humble cabin boy discovered a truth that we shy away from like a razor-blade: the gift of suffering and a knowledge of God can go hand in hand.

If we dare to imagine the mind of God the Father, we must conclude that he faces an agonizing dilemma. When his children are comfortable they do not seek the coming of the kingdom. Instead, they indulge in a deep spiritual lethargy. "Fortunate people seldom mend their ways," La Rochefoucauld pointed out, "for when good luck crowns their misdeeds with success, they think it is because they are right."[11] Religious duties may be performed by these people, but often out of habit. The existence of God is debated idly in cafes, as an intellectual amusement. Or a declaration may be made that "I am an agnostic" because "we can never know whether there is a God or not." God the Father cannot enter such a soul, stifled as it is with boredom or pride. He waits humbly outside, hoping to be called in. But he may have to wait a long time. When hardship enters the picture, it rots the iron-willed ego and creates a fresh taste for the riches of spirituality. At last, God the Father is asked to enter this newly opened, aching heart. And so, the divine parent is left with the painful choice of remaining hidden, or inflicting pain on his children to make them grow in their awareness of him and of their own deeper nature.

Jesus makes the same point in the New Testament. He speaks to a man who has kept the commandments faithfully all his life, but remains rich:

> "There is still one thing lacking. Sell all that you own and distribute the money to the poor, and you will have treasure in heaven; then come, follow me." But when [the rich man] heard this he became sad; for he was very rich. Jesus looked at him and said, "How hard it is for those who have wealth to enter the kingdom of God!" Luke 18:22-24

And, conversely, how much easier it is to find the kingdom for those who endure pain heroically?

But why are some people given a massive dose of this burden-cum-gift called pain, and some not? It's because pain often reaches us by a "caprice of fate," and that's not all bad. The thunderclap of misfortune comforts us with the knowledge that there is a divine mind at work, one that is so much greater than ours, with purposes we can never understand. This mystery liberates us from the tyranny of our intellects and from the way we crave an explanation and a nostrum for every twinge of discomfort. Where there is no insight into our "fate" and the pain it delivers, there is ample room for faith, or for cynicism. And this is another God-given opportunity for us to snatch out of the jaws of suffering. As a wise person once said, "An optimist sees the opportunity in every difficulty. A pessimist sees the difficulty in every opportunity."

In the real world outside Eden, pain and hardship are much more to us than a nasty, hand-me-down punishment for Adam and Eve's sin. But in a certain sense, Genesis is still right. We know that "the wages of sin is death." We also know that pain can draw a sinful person back into a spiritual life. So Genesis is right on the button. We would not need the spiritual exaltation that follows pain if we did not first debase ourselves through sin. In that sense, pain is God's great gift to the sinful Adam and Eve outside the garden, not his curse.

Death: The Third "Curse" of Adam and Eve

Life is the silken bond between our bodies and something deliciously mysterious that lies beyond in the world of the spirit. Life is the power to appreciate beauty, which is always personal, even when the splendor is as remote as the mountains or as timeless as the sea. Life is the yearning to love God and our neighbors—in so far as we may know anything about them. Life is the drive to make life go on forever.

Death devastates families. It takes away the ones we love—if they are children, with unbearable pain. Death is the vile tool of murderers. It turns the beautiful living body into a putrefaction that reeks with horror. Death casts a pall over the site of battles for years or for centuries and darkens the mood in hospital wards. Death appears to have nothing to recommend it. How can it have, when it takes away people like Ludwig van Beethoven and

"Precious Doe," the unnamed little black girl who was killed, beheaded, and thrown away in a Southern U.S. city?[12]

The answer is that there is a lot to be said in favor of death, in principle, both in nature and in the world of human society.

We die for a hundred thousand reasons: avalanches and accidents, drowning and draughts, leopard attacks and lightning strikes, yaws and yellow fever. Internally, everybody harbors time bombs, such as spina bifida or genes that bring cancer in later life. These killers are all a consequence of the finite nature of the universe, just like the need to work. Everything in the universe, from a supernova to a pebble and from a diatom to an atomizer, must occupy a limited space for a limited time. And all living creatures have to be born, endure a certain life span, and die. Otherwise they would be infinite.

Death is not only a consequence of the world's finitude. It is also a key component of the Creator's housekeeping strategy. Lions, bee eaters, and hyenas all live by killing and eating other animals. Each defecates and restores the remains of its meal to the world of plants, which grow heartily and are eaten by other animals, starting the life-and-death cycle all over again. The elegance of this morbid arrangement is that there is no garbage left behind. The horror of death supports life, cleanly, in a finite cosmos.

We would all live in a weird, misbegotten universe if its natural resources were not husbanded through death. The animals of this fantasy world would not kill one another for food. They would prance around as immortal as unicorns. The joy of birth would be unknown because it would overcrowd the world of undying animals. And a ten-mile-wide shower of food would have to travel to Earth from outer space for millions of years to continuously feed all the undying creatures, unless they didn't eat at all. In this fantastical world, miracles would become commonplace. God the Father would be obliged to create all the world's creatures by fiat at the beginning, move the trillions of tons of food from space by his divine will, ship out all the waste by some kind of "magic," and then destroy all the animals at the end, if there was an end. From time to time, in this bizarre world, God the Father would have to overrule his own scientific laws. The infinite would become inextricably mixed up with the finite. The miraculous would comingle with the mundane.

God the Father has chosen not to order nature by frequent personal intervention. He has created a set of iron scientific laws and stood back from them. He is apparently too humble to play the emperor and intimidate the human race with spectacular cosmic displays of raining edibles or confuse it with shifting scientific laws that satisfy his whims. God the Father remains shyly invisible, like a child at an adult's birthday party. He hides behind the screen of a predictable nature, which allows us to reliably grow food and make the medicines we need with some independence. But his creative work shines out like a flare. His artist's palette carries all the colors of birth and death, and much more besides. With his mystical brushes he is always creating new beauty in the fantastic creatures that come and go in the world, and in the lovely moving forms of the waves, the sand dunes, the meadows, and the mountains. And at the core of God the Father's magnificent creation stands pain and death in all their glory.

Death has many spiritual benefits as well, just like pain. It keeps human society clean because it decisively conquers the evil that arises from our sins. It is death that silences zealots, defeats hostile armies, and removes people who are unable to advance their archaic thinking in keeping with the needs of the times. Death is the foundation of the community's ongoing journey out of evil into a creative life.

The problem with evil is that it is always seductive, even for the righteous. In the fourth and fifth centuries, the threat to the coming of God's kingdom was heresy—attractive but false interpretations of God's word. The theological disputes at that time were tumultuous but are barely recalled forty generations later, except in dry church textbooks. In the Middle Ages, evil seemed to take the form of witchcraft. But the greater evil was the torture and murder of thousands of solitary women, falsely alleged to be hags. Witchcraft and what it cruelly cloaked, church-sanctioned murder, vanished in later generations and is barely comprehensible to the modern mind. In the twentieth century, evil transformed itself into a battle between communism and capitalism, both evil to the other's adherents. But the greater threat was the destruction of the human race by nuclear war.

In the twenty-first century, evil is terrorism for the West, and for Muslims, the perversion of the great religion of Islam into an ideological tool of hatred and murder. Evil confounds the best of us, but it does not grow in human history. "Do not fret because of evildoers," the Bible says, "Do not envy the wicked; for the evil have no future; the lamp of the wicked will go out" (Proverbs 24:19-20). Evil dies with each generation and is brought back in a new, completely unexpected form until it is conquered by death and decency once again. Evil uses death as its weapon, but death is also its most implacable enemy.

Wisdom grows undiminished by death. Medicine has made great advances, so has science, education, and theology, despite the generations of good, hardworking people who have toiled in these fields and passed away. In the twenty-first century, there is a better understanding of God than ever before, probably in all religions. And this will likely be even truer in the twenty-second century. Wisdom flowers through all the seasons of humankind. It lays down ever deeper roots and guides the community toward the kingdom of God. The handmaiden of the flowering of wisdom is the death of evil people. Society does cleanse itself by other mechanisms, but God the Father's gift of death is the most effective.

Jesus's vision of heaven seems to confirm this view of death as social therapy. Some Sadducees approached him and told him about a woman who had married seven men. "Which would be her husband in the after life?" they asked, hoping to confound him. Jesus replied: "Those who belong to this age marry and are given in marriage; but those who are considered worthy of a place in that age and in the resurrection from the dead neither marry nor are given in marriage. Indeed, they cannot die anymore, because they are like angels and are children of God, being children of the resurrection" (Luke 20:34-36). People of "the other world" do not marry because there is no need to give birth and replace people taken by death. There is no need for death because there is no sin and no evil to conquer—the inhabitants are all worthy "sons and daughters of God." In this world that we live in, death is not a punishment for sin, as Genesis suggests. Death is the God-given mechanism that saves us from all the evils of our sins. But Genesis is partly right. It is sin that made death and its benefits necessary.

The paradox of death—the end we dread—is that it gives life its brilliance. Living would soon lose its piquancy if it could go on forever. We would chronically procrastinate, because there would always be time later—lots of time—to do any particular job. The beauty of the natural world would lose its edge because it would be always there for us to gaze at, for eons. The sunset we are now afraid we'll miss or the spider's web bejeweled with dew that we look for so eagerly some mornings, would lose their power to charm if we knew we could see them, again and again, reliably, for thirty thousand years. The enjoyment of life is always founded on surprise, the certainty of fresh change, and a pace of living driven by the conviction of an imminent end to everything through death. Those people who seek the Fountain of Youth do not understand life. Without imminent death, there would be little spice to living. The Fountain of Youth would inflict a sentence of terminal boredom on the beneficiary. A death that will come soon is an integral part of God the Father's most precious gift of life.

Death is the most ascendant of all adventures, one usually reserved with justice for those who have no adventures left in them as they lie confined to their aged deathbed, preparing to travel to the far country. For the terminally ill, death is a light that approaches, as their loved ones live in its gathering shadow. Death is the portal between a life we barely understand and one that we do not know at all. "Not one returns to tell us of the Road, Which to discover we must travel too,"[13] says Omar Khayyam. How can we condemn death? Death defeats the evil of Adam and Eve's sin. Death is the frame that highlights life's picture. Without death there would be no life worth living.

The Father's Blessings—the Freedom to Love

God the Father confers many favors on the human race, not just the three putative "curses." And Genesis itself acknowledges some of these blessings. In the garden, "the soil produced all such trees as charm the eye and satisfy the taste." Clearly, we are capable of both aesthetic and gustatory pleasure. But also a lot more. Two great gifts that Genesis fails to mention are artistic creativity and a sense of fun. But the greatest gift of all is the freedom to love.

Love is as fragile as life. It is only love when it is freely given and can be taken away, in the same way that life is intensified by the threat of death. Love can never be coerced. It is always a living thing and must be chosen freely minute by minute by the lover, in preference to the alternative—rejection of the person loved. Love is quintessentially human, but it is not finite. Love lies in the realm of both the human and the infinite, because the laws of love apparently bind the Creator as well. God the Father loves, too, in much the same way that we love. And despite his awesome power, God the Father does not command us to love him back. Perhaps he cannot, because of love's free nature. Perhaps God the Father has to court us and hope that he can earn our love, like any woman making herself beautiful for her man. The love of God's children for God the Father will follow, he hopes, poignantly. But if we are to love God the Father we must exercise the freedom to love or to hate that he has given us in such abundance.

The Freedom to Hate

After the September 11, 2001, terrorist attacks on New York City, which killed more than three thousand people, Mohamed Elmasry, president of the Canadian Islamic Congress, uttered a commonly heard cry: "How can God allow innocent people to die? Couldn't God do something about it? How can the Creator allow people to commit murder under the divine name?"[14] The answer is often glibly given, yet at the same time it is unfathomable. God the Father wants us to love him, and love can only be freely given, so he has endowed all of us with the freedom to love or to hate to our heart's content. And that is another truth found in the Garden of Eden. Adam and Eve are told not to eat the forbidden fruit, but they are free to do what they want. God the Father places a higher value on human freedom than he does on our obedience to him.

This idea of a divine gift of free will is laughable to those who scorn the notion of a loving God. Where was this "divine gift" in 1985, they sneer, when thousands of people died on an island off Bangladesh that was swept clean by a tidal wave? The island's inhabitants were so poor they were not even recognized by the Bangladeshi government, which reported the place was uninhabited. In fact, this small strip of land was home to ten thousand families that had nowhere else to go. They squatted on the island because it had just emerged from the sea and was covered with fertile silt that could grow crops. Each family knew the risks. A storm had killed twenty thousand people along the same coast, fifteen years earlier. But these families were the poorest of the poor, trying to make a living in a place nobody else would dare to occupy. In the midst of this dreadful adventure, they relied on frequent prayer and on a deep devotion to God, as only the poor will do.

The tidal wave swept the island clean of buildings, livestock, and people, leaving only a few naked bodies that soon became bloated with rot. Nature, which is designed by God the Father, treated these dirt-poor people with contempt and erased them from the face of the earth. What happened to their free will, we might ask. Was it trumped by the malevolent will of God? Many people would shout Yes! It is the so-called God the Father, they would say, who creates a world in which poverty is endured by so many good people. He is the one who lets loose the killer cyclones and their waves. If he is omnipotent, let him find another way to make rain in the Bay of Bengal! That's if he really cares, of course.

If we stand back and look at the broader picture, it is even more horrific. In the Soviet Union from 1918 to 1952, Vladimir Lenin and Joseph Stalin murdered 40 million–60 million people, according to Russian authorities.[15] The victims were either worked to death or shot or starved. In the 1940s, Hitler killed another 40 million people by unleashing World War II. His gas chambers destroyed 6 million Jews, gypsies, and gays. That's a total of 100 million people murdered in Europe alone in the twentieth century. In Asia, there are the approximately 100 million people massacred in Cambodia, in the Japanese-Chinese war, and in other atrocities. That's a horrendous tally of mass murder for theologians and their pals to explain away.

The solemn truth is that God the Father did provide for the victims of these massacres—by proxy, through the free will given to each one of us all over the world. In the same month as the killer cyclone, an American contractor was caught selling thousands of ashtrays to the U.S. military for $660 apiece, far beyond their worth. This contractor's greed misappropriated millions of dollars that could have been assigned by the U.S. government as aid to the Bangladeshi people, before the storm. Other wealthy nations were indifferent to the Bangladeshis' plight and continued their internal policies of building the wealth of their already wealthy citizens. The affluent West also turned its back on the barbarism that was ruining Afghanistan in the 1990s, until it was stung into paying attention by the September 11, 2001, attacks. After that, a conference of First World countries poured aid into Afghanistan, out of self-defense rather than caring. That flow of aid began to peter out within months.

All religions tell us that God does not want Cambodians or Siberians to die at the hands of evil men. Their deaths flow from the way we all use our freedom of choice. And that's the answer to this troubling conundrum. Don't blame God. Blame our own free choices. We always have the means to help—and we do not. But this answer doesn't satisfy our hunger for a deeper theological response to the sheer horror of the 200 million killings in the twentieth century. Why didn't God the Father intervene to stop the carnage? Surely he can find a way to save so many people—some way that is compatible with natural law, or theology, or whatever his problem happens to be? Once again, we fall back on the conclusion that free will is a total and absolute gift. We can do anything we want with it—at any cost to God the Father or to ourselves, his children. That's why God really is a Father. He treats his children as young adults and allows them to grow up. Any good father shudders and closes his eyes to his adult children's choices, but they must be allowed to live their own lives and make their own mistakes. If the father intervenes, he will damage them. The paradox of evil is that if God prevented us from going down that dark, mournful path, we would become little more than his divine puppets, devoid of our own free will and our own dignity.

This argument is all very well, as far as it goes, but there is still a dark mystery to so much mass murder, one that we cannot quite reach with all these handy explanations. Does it in the end mean that there really is no God? We ask ourselves, wracked by doubt. Is the idea that God is a loving Father just a bit of theological flimflam? The Jews who have lived through the Holocaust have the greatest right to speak on this question. They teach us most solemnly that the pall of spiritual darkness hanging over that abomination is still not a justification for atheism. The Holocaust has become the blackest and most challenging touchstone of the modern Jewish faith, a very somber spiritual treasure for which the Jews have paid a high price. But for all its horror, the memory of the Holocaust is a spiritual possession nevertheless. Jews of the most noble spirituality know that somehow or other it does not negate the existence of a caring God.

It is easy to condemn God the Father for all the horrific agonies we inflict upon one another. But we only ever see half the picture. God the Father remains invisible during our deadly rampages and our self-serving blasphemies against him. But if we believe Jesus when he talks about God the Father's love, we might speculate that the children's suffering is more painful to the Father than it ever is to the children. And perhaps that is the answer to the dilemma of the Holocaust. It was painful to the Jews, but how much more painful was it to God, the Father of his chosen people? If we knew the heavy "emotional suffering" that God must endure to preserve our freedom, we might be less ready to condemn him.

God the Father's Blessings—a Sense of Fun

There's much more to life than hatred, death, and discomfort. As Crowfoot suggested, there is also fun, which is one of the treasures we find when we root around in the overflowing hamper of gifts given to all of us at birth. Fun is more than pleasure or a good joke. Fun is the ability to conquer pain and hardship by means of play. The Berlin Wall stood for twenty-eight years, harshly dividing East Germany and West Germany and preventing the people of East Germany from escaping Soviet oppression. It was demolished in 1989 as a prelude to the unification of Germany. But before it was taken down, it was conquered—by fun. A man rode his bicycle along the top of the wall for no other purpose than to get on top of it. Then it was demoted to any old wall by young people writing graffiti all over it with spray cans. Others hit the wall with hammers in a mock demolition, just for the fun of it. By the time fun had spoken, this monument to despotism was doomed.

In Kabul in 2001, the most touching sign of the end of the Taliban tyranny was the sight of children flying kites in a park—good fun proclaimed the end of a bad scene. In offices everywhere, men and women talk and laugh among themselves as they perform tedious tasks in insurance or journalism or nursing. The play of fun softens the weight of the work while enhancing productivity. Fun can even conquer illness. "A man paralyzed with ankylosing spondulitis and given only a few months to live checked himself out of hospital, and into a hotel room where he consumed mega doses of Vitamin C and watched a long series of Laurel and Hardy movies. His paralysis went away."[16] Fun is triumphant even over dying. All tyrants try to outlaw fun, because it is part of God the Father's gift of human freedom. Fun reminds us that life is not a "curse," as Genesis would have us believe.

When We Say "Father"

All this inquiry into life and death and the meaning of pain and sorrow can be subsumed into one reverent genuflection to God by beginning to say Jesus's prayer. But what is the character of this pregnant first word, "Father," gleaming at the head of the prayer? One theologian calls it the "title" and leaves it out of the list of requests like "Thy Kingdom Come" and "Forgive us" and "Lead us." The word Father is definitely not a petition, we are told. It is merely the identity of the one to whom all the other petitions are addressed. But this view is too antiseptic. It ignores the subtle play of Trinity in the prayer, with the Father overarching all but giving rise to the High Priest and the King. Clearly, Father is more than God's title. It is a petition that God the Father will help the community of his children to build its relationship with him, the Father. This conclusion is inescapable because the whole of Jesus's prayer tells us we can do nothing without God's help, not even hallow his name or call upon his kingdom.

We have to ask God to help us to do all these things. So every word we say to God in this prayer must be a petition, including the word *Father,* which is a plea to help us understand where we came from and where we belong.

"Father" begs the divine parent to court this petulant son or daughter into loving him. "Father, hug us," it says, "and put your arms around us, so that we will hug you, too." "Father" is an entreaty that we recognize all other people in the world as family. We no longer want to treat them as biological material, to be snubbed or robbed or ruled. We want to learn that the Great Designer of the universe is bound to every one of his children by love. We beg him to help us master the lesson that he who made the stars and the atom stoops down to love cyclists, psychiatrists, and psychopaths. When we say "Father," we want all human lives to become, to us, the most sacred property of the Creator. "Father" asks God to open our hearts to this brilliant, life-giving reality.

To say "Father" is to beg to become a child again and throw off all the weary experiences of an adult. To say "Father" is to embrace the great high God through all the teeming distractions in our coarse, turbulent lives. To say "Father" is to journey to God like a Polynesian navigator, with family and chickens in the canoe, determined to get home to the sacred island over the horizon, or perish in the vast ocean. To say "Father" is to battle our way toward God like a warrior, through a fog of pain and the terror of death, with all the humility of self-sacrifice. To say "Father" is to ask to be allowed to go to the source of life like a lover, free to quarrel, but always with impassioned loyalty.

"Father" is a greeting from a child to a parent that gets warmer each time it is spoken. It begins as a salute from far away, out of a swamp of selfishness. "Father, I'm trying to get out of this mess. Please be patient with me." Then "Father" becomes the cry of the prodigal son after the inheritance has been squandered and he has returned home. "Father, I've come back. Let me work as one of your servants. I'm not worthy to be your son." When the Father's whoop of welcome from an open window drowns out the son's confession, "Father!" changes to a joyous call on arrival at the front door, eager to see the beloved parent within. "Dad, I'm home!" Then "Father" becomes a hug as Father and child come together once again after their long separation. Finally, for those who consider all their actions in a spiritual light, "Father" becomes a total surrender to a loving God who is always present in their lives and is never forgotten.

3

Hallowed Be Thy Name

A city woman walks in the forest enjoying the colors of nature, but she cannot distinguish the various plants. It's all a beautiful blur, punctuated by nameless birds and flowers. To enhance her pleasure, she takes a course in botany. She is told about the beech, the oak, and the honey locust. As she passes each tree she notes the difference—the oak has dentate leaves, the beech has a smooth bark, the honey locust has feathery leaves. She discovers that knowing the name for a tree is the beginning of knowledge of the tree itself. It is the same with people. To know a person's name is to start to know the person. We may be able to identify the man down the street by his beard and the way he walks, but he remains a mystery until we can say "Good morning, Mr. Anderson!" To know a person's name is to start to know what the community knows: who he is and who his antecedents were.

"Hallowed be thy name" is a prayer that everybody knows and respects God's name. That does not mean we learn to spell G-O-D. It means we come to know and cherish who God really is. Of course, the one true God is unknowable. Philosophers have tried for centuries to define him or her or it in vain. They express the futility of the exercise with elegant phrases, such as "God is a process or a verb, rather than a noun." Or "God is an idea we can imagine, but never express" (which doesn't help much).

They even pay tribute to a once-upon-a-time belief in God with nihilism, such as Friedrich Nietzsche's "God is dead."[1] But God's sacred character can be known insofar as it has been revealed—how he appeared in the community, what he has done for us, and what he expects us to do in return. Once we know God's character or "name," we can distinguish the real God from all the other gods, and we can develop the appropriate respect by "hallowing [God's] name."

Who Is God?

Almost all peoples have worshiped a supreme being who embodies elements of the one supreme God that we know today through Jesus and the Israelites. Among the ancient Greeks, the top god was Zeus, who was called the "father of gods and men" but was not a loving father, nor the maker of the natural world. His counterpart among the natives of North America is the Great Spirit, who created reality and is benign but is not called "Father." In Polynesia, the supreme god was Kane. In ancient Egypt, it was the Sun. Australian aborigines, many African peoples, and the Druids knew of a supreme being. In fact, belief in a supreme god was a universal phenomenon among ancient people, even though they had no contact with one another. This core theological awareness flowed from within humanity itself or from a human perception of the world, or it was born during the human race's infancy, when all people lived close to one another and shared the same world experience. Whatever the reason, visceral belief in a creator is held by the whole human race and speaks about our spiritual nature.

Ancient people also believed in spirits, demons, and junior gods, which were constructed out of the phenomena of nature or the content of dreams. In the Middle East, people worshipped Baal and Dagon and many other gods, some of whom refused to promote the fertility of crops until the work of temple prostitutes had been completed or some precious thing had been burnt in sacrifice. The ancient Greek historian Herodotus wrote about such worship in Assyria. A woman, even a society matron, was obliged to spend time in the temple until she had been mounted. Some of that city's less comely women spent three or four years waiting to be released by the lustful kindness of a stranger.[2] Moloch, the god of the Canaanites, demanded the sacrifice of children before he would enhance the fortunes of their parents. The Incas killed children to send their spirits as messengers to plead with gods for their blessings on the community.

All people need to worship something—anything—and that basic drive will not be denied. Even atheists, agnostics, and the spiritually indifferent still worship something. False deities are few but there are still idols aplenty. Booze helps some people smother their need to worship God by blotting out their higher human sensitivities. In extreme cases, the booze becomes the idol. Others copulate with many partners. Sex is the anodyne, but the subtle lure is that sex is the only human activity that plumbs both our animal and spiritual natures at the same time. Hard work engages the obsessions of some people. They labor seven days a week, worshiping a god that is insatiable. It's fashionable to believe that workaholism is a psychological defect, but it's more likely a spiritual one.

Democracy or capitalism are potent idols for modern Westerners who believe that these ideologies by themselves will save the world. Others worship a human institution and cruelly sacrifice the individual at that altar. Kenneth Westhues, a distinguished sociologist at the University of Waterloo, Ontario, has documented the way many university administrators around the world have destroyed the reputations of staff members by corrupt "legal" procedures because their victims have allegedly embarrassed the sacred institution. A few people worship power, the powerful illusion that God is "me."

High philosophies are not safe, either. They, too, project many gods. To deists, God is remote—he made the universe and stands apart. This leaves a lot of room for the worship of more mundane idols who are present in the world around us. The great scientist Albert Einstein believed the universe was God, and each person was an ant-like part of this vast deity. The question is whether the universe then becomes an idol for an Einstein or not. A few people admit the existence of the one real immanent God, but attribute unholiness to him. To Islamic extremists, God welcomes into paradise those people who kill themselves while blowing up innocent victims. There are similar gods in the Christianity practiced in Northern Ireland and in the Judaism and Islam practiced in parts of the Middle East. God has many names to many people, some of them quite foul.

The Real Name of God

Everybody knows the Creator insofar as they can discern him through the beauty of the natural world received with a humble and clean heart. That's especially true of the native people of North America and Australia. But there is more to God than the sublime spirituality of his creation. There is also theology that identifies the people to whom God has spoken, and explores the message they pass on. This inquiry is laborious for anybody who wants to give the right person the sacred respect that is his due by hallowing his name.

The first task for the ancient Hebrews was to distinguish the real God from all the false gods and idols that seduced the world at that time. Moses learned the most basic distinction when God spoke to him on Mount Sinai. "Moses said to God, 'If I come to the Israelites and say to them "The God of your ancestors has sent me to you," and they ask me, "What is his name?" what shall I say to them?' God said to Moses, 'I am who I am'" (Exodus 3:13-14). In other words, I am the God that exists. All the other gods are those that "are not." The God of Moses was also saying other things in this passage, such as: "Look, I am who I am, and you can never know me." He was also saying: "I AM in the eternal present, folded within the past and the future." Jesus echoed this last reading when he said: "Very truly, I tell you, before Abraham was, I am" (John 8:58). Knowing God's timelessness is a beginning, but it is not enough to hallow God's name safely.

God's Nicknames

The human encyclopedia of the divine contains many caricatures of the One True God that have been drawn by holy men and women, who were perhaps inspired, but who saw only a small part of God's identity. That's why God's character keeps changing, even in Scripture, where he is always the same God.

At first, in the Old Testament, God the Father appears to be a person who shows little mercy. He destroys Sodom and Gomorrah in a cataclysm of nuclear proportions for a crime that is either unloving "sodomy" or rape or violation of hospitality, depending on the theologian consulted. God rescues Lot, even after the man has offered his two virginal daughters to the mob to slake its lust. On the journey to the mountains, Lot's wife looks back at the burning cities, and God eliminates her. Lot was the only half-decent man in Sodom, and presumably his wife was also well-behaved. But in a flash, she becomes a pillar of salt that is washed into the Dead Sea when the rains come. Lot is not even left with a corpse to mourn over. God eliminates not only the woman, but even her identity (the Bible gives her no name)—for petty insubordination. Safe in the mountains, believing they are the only people left alive, Lot's daughters get their father drunk and inseminate themselves upon him.

What is this story and what bearing does it have on any search we make for God the Father's identity? The starting point is a recognition that the Bible is not only theology and history, it is also literature. Its divinely inspired writers use many engaging devices (particularly well-told stories) to deliver a vast, subtle, and profound message that would never be read if it was presented as a theological treatise or a dry literal history. That's why the Bible's books change in character from one to the other to reveal the flowering of God's name in the world.

The first book, Genesis, contains many such stories, starting with the creation account in the Garden of Eden, where sin brings death, and the story of Methuselah, whose virtue allowed him to live almost one thousand years. In the story of Noah, a flood covers the entire earth, and later a tower reaches to heaven. There's no intention to pass these stories off as fact. The author makes that clear. "And God said, 'Let there be a dome in the midst of the waters, and let it separate the waters from the waters.' So God made the dome and separated the waters that were under the dome from the waters that were above the dome. And it was so. God called the dome Sky" (Genesis 1:6-8). Genesis does not really insist that there are billions of tons of water resting on top of the sky and piddling through as rain. These stories capture the sense that we are viewing ancient events dimly through the great magnifying mists of the past. The legend of Sodom and Lot offers the same simple lesson as that of Adam and Eve: disobedience against God brings terrible consequences. One clue to its legendary character is the heroic manhood of Lot. What other man could inseminate a woman while passed out in a drunken stupor, not once but twice?

God the Father, destroyer of worlds, becomes kinder through the years. In the Ten Commandments, handed down to Moses in about 1250 B.C., God threatens to punish the offspring of those who worship idols, but only to the "third or fourth generation"—not forever, as in the case of Adam and Eve's sin. But can this be the all-loving God the Father revealed by Jesus? What about the human rights of the "three or four generations" of descendants of idol worshipers, then and now? The son of Martin Bormann, the wicked secretary to Adolf Hitler, worked as a missionary in Africa with the poorest of the poor and later lectured on the evils of Nazism.[3] Is there no relief available to such a son for his father's idolatry?

In Exodus, the great legends peter out, but God the Father still falls into a terrible rage once in a while, even urging his chosen people to commit merciless genocide:

> When the Lord your God brings you into the land that you are about to enter and occupy, and he clears away many nations before you—the Hittites, the Girgashites, the Amorites, the Canaanites, the Perizzites, the Hivites, and the Jebusites, seven nations mightier and more numerous than you—and when the Lord your God gives them over to you and you defeat them, then you must utterly destroy them. Make no covenant with them and show them no mercy. Deuteronomy 7:1-2

In some cases, a conquered nations' women can be "married," apparently without their consent. "Suppose you see among the captives a beautiful woman whom you desire and want to marry... [she] shall remain in your house a full month, mourning for her father and mother [whom you have slaughtered]; after that you may go in to her and be her husband, and she shall be your wife" (Deuteronomy 21:11-13).

This is not just idle posturing. God the Father flies into a fury when his orders are flouted. God's mouthpiece, the prophet Samuel, tells King Saul: "Now go and attack Amalek, and utterly destroy all that they have; do not spare them, but kill both man and woman, child and infant, ox and sheep, camel and donkey" (1 Samuel 15:3). Saul goes out and slaughters the Amalekites—all but one. He spares King Agag, probably out of a sense of noblesse oblige. Saul also keeps some of the Amalekites' goats and oxen, so that his soldiers may sacrifice them to the Lord God. But God does not see Saul's conduct as an act of mercy, or reverence for him. He sees it only as defiance. Samuel tells Saul: "Because you have rejected the word of the Lord, he has also rejected you from being king" (1 Samuel 15:23). Samuel then anoints the future king, David. The remainder of Saul's reign is wracked with jealousy of David.

The God depicted here is hardly a loving Father. He takes on the clothes of a terrible tyrant. The consequence of such a harsh depiction is that while God chose to be the God of all nations through the Hebrew people (Genesis 12:1-3), in many passages he appears to be only the partisan Father of the Hebrew people.

These ancient passages raise troubling questions about this God we try to hallow.

The question is whether this Old Testament image of God is for "spiritual juveniles" who need to grow up or whether it is mature but incomplete. The answer may be that the early Bible books insist on everybody's submission to God's rule and report his terrible punishments against any rebels because a people's first lesson is to obey God and fear him. And that's the paradox of the fear of God—it brings great peace to the individual (not anxiety) and thereby lays a firm foundation for the divine law, which sets the people apart as God's holy ones.

Another reality leaping out of the Bible is that the God we think we know always reflects the society in which we live. The genocidal God of Exodus is a stark necessity for the nation of 600,000 people moving across the desert floor toward the promised land, which they will seize from its occupants. This moving, homeless host threatened all the surrounding nations and had to deal mercilessly with them to preserve its identity. It needed the blessings of the one true God of war. When the Israelites are settled, God will show a kinder face.

The Many "God the Fathers" of Christianity

Even the Christian churches have twisted the character of God the Father to their own ends, and that's a tragedy, considering they enjoy the benefit of Jesus's once-and-for-all teaching. The Dutch Reformed Church of South Africa provided the theological justification for apartheid—teaching that the Bible says blacks are a lesser people. The Protestant churches of Northern Ireland turned a blind eye to their adherents' bigotry against Catholics for years. Catholics could not get jobs, and the few that found work could not get promotion. There are other defects in other versions of the Christian faith.

So how is any modern Christian to know God the Father more fully as we proceed toward hallowing his name? Do we read the Bible diligently and discern God the Father's character all by ourselves like the woman in the forest naming trees? No, because we ourselves are a human lens that will always distort the divine vision. What we must do is listen carefully to the community of the church. At the same time, with humility, we must strip away everything from the church's teaching that is a defective human overlay and obscures the real name of God—and there are as many human overlays as there are skins on an onion. Stripping them away is not easy, and it might take a lifetime. But Jesus's prayer tells us that it must be done, because we must hallow God's name cleanly.

The Final Prophet

Why do so many conflicting snapshots of the one true God turn up through the ages? The answer appears to be that almost all human activity is tainted with self. That's true of the works of laypeople and politicians, philanthropists and philosophers, doctors and bricklayers. In religion itself, God's word is often garbled by the human character of prophets and priests, either because they are irresponsible or venal, or because they can only shape their view of the divine out of the culture of the times. God the Father's real character awaits unveiling by the final prophet, Jesus, who is both human like the prophets, and much more than human.

The key role of this final prophet is explained by God obliquely to his inspired writers, early on for all to read. This occurs when Moses and Aaron lead the Israelites out of Egypt toward the promised land. The two prophets are not allowed to complete the journey because their appreciation of God's holiness is defective—as it is for all humans. "But the Lord said to Moses and Aaron, 'Because you did not trust in me, to show my holiness before the eyes of the Israelites, therefore you shall not bring this assembly into the land that I have given them'" (Numbers 20:12). Scholars do not agree on the specific "sin" committed by Moses and Aaron. But whatever it was, this passage also points to the broader theological incompetence that arises out of their humanness.

The Israelites reach the border of the promised land, and Moses tells the Israelites that another will lead them across:

> When Moses had finished speaking all these words to all Israel, he said to them: "I am now one hundred twenty years old. I am no longer able to get about, and the Lord has told me, 'You shall not cross over this Jordan.' The Lord your God himself will cross over before you. He will destroy these nations before you, and you shall dispossess them. Joshua also will cross over before you, as the Lord promised." Deuteronomy 31:1-3

The name "Joshua" is equivalent to "Jesus." And what "Joshua/Jesus" leads Israel and the human race into is the promised land of the Israelites, which is prophetic of the kingdom of God.

Joshua leads Israel into the promised land, but Jesus alone is capable of leadership of the holy nation into God's kingdom. That's because no other human being has the divine insight—not Moses, nor Aaron, nor Samuel, nor any of the Old Testament prophets or leaders of the Christian churches. "Not that anyone has seen the Father except the one who is from God; he has seen the Father," Jesus says (John 6:46). And only Jesus can portray the Father's true character and give us his name to hallow.

The Stage Is Set

The Old Testament's portrayal of the true God becomes less fierce and more subtle as the Bible develops. The desert's bellicose God becomes a God of paradox, whose veiled face arises out of the spiritual introspection forced on the Israelites when they are conquered by Babylon, or threatened by the hordes of Assyria. This holy nation needs a savior, but because this is God's nation, the savior will be both political and spiritual. So, mystery and circumlocution arise in the sacred writings. God will still conquer on behalf of his people, but not by force of arms over nations like the Amalekites and the Perizzites. God's new victory will be the conquest of the world, and it will last forever. This brilliant, piercing wisdom flows from the sorrow of Israel's defeat, in the way that hardship and pain can always bring their own unique spirituality.

In the seventh century before Christ, the prophets start to talk of a noble king and a suffering servant, who are apparently the same person. "Therefore the Lord himself will give you a sign," the prophet Isaiah says. "Look, the young woman is with child and shall bear a son, and shall name him Immanuel [God is with us]" (Isaiah 7:14). Later Isaiah adds: "For a child has been born for us, a son given to us; authority rests upon his shoulders; and he is named Wonderful Counselor, Mighty God, Everlasting Father, Prince of Peace" (Isaiah 9:6). The person that comes is a divine male child (called "Mighty God"), who will counsel us. Isaiah also quotes the Lord as saying:

> "See, my servant shall prosper; he shall be exalted and lifted up, and shall be very high. Just as there were many who were astonished at him—so marred was his appearance, beyond human semblance, and his form beyond that of mortals—so he shall startle many nations; kings shall shut their mouths because of him; for that which had not been told them they

shall see, and that which they had not heard they shall contemplate."
Isaiah 52:13-15

The interpretation of these passages passes through different fashions from time to time. The child and the servant-king may have been real people alive in Isaiah's time. But these words also establish a prophesy of Jesus "the king," who was "marred" by humiliation and pain while "lifted" on the cross, but who succeeded in his mission to "counsel" the world as to the face of God the Father.

Jeremiah drops the second shoe: "The days are surely coming, says the Lord, when I shall raise up for David a righteous Branch [a successor], and he shall reign as king and deal wisely, and shall execute justice and righteousness in the land. In his days Judah will be saved and Israel will live in safety. And this is the name by which he will be called: 'The Lord is our righteousness'" (Jeremiah 23:5-6). Jeremiah's words may refer to a person of his time, but he also seems to be conjuring up the prophesy of Nathan to King David, made many years earlier: "Your house and your kingdom shall be made sure forever before me; your throne shall be established forever" (2 Samuel 7:16). The righteous King who finally brings justice to the land and saves Israel will be a successor of David.

Jeremiah makes an important distinction about God's saving work:

> Therefore, the days are surely coming, says the Lord, when it shall no longer be said, "As the Lord lives who brought the people of Israel up out of the land of Egypt," but "As the Lord lives who brought out and led the offspring of the house of Israel out of the land of the north and out of all the lands where he had driven them." Then they shall live in their own land.
> Jeremiah 23:7-8

When God rescued the Israelites from bondage in Egypt, they had not heard the divine word that was delivered to Moses in the journey through the desert. Therefore, bondage in Egypt is symbolic of sin in a state of ignorance of the law. When the Israelites had settled in the promised land, all their sins were committed in full knowledge of the Ten Commandments and other divine prophecy. Jeremiah says that God drove the Israelites into alien lands as a punishment for this defiance. When God rescues his people from "the north country" where he drove them, Jeremiah implies, this will be deliverance from full, knowing sin, not just a liberation from bondage. God will have graduated from rescuer to redeemer. The upshot of all this prophesy is that the Messiah will be a servant, one who will suffer, and one who will be a king descended from David. He will lead his people out of exile and he will redeem them from sin.

Israel's second monarch, King David, was the most successful of all Israel's kings. He was spiritually noble, at least at first. He was a great poet and a great warrior who expanded Israel's borders from the edge of Egypt to the river Euphrates, just as far as the Lord God had promised Abram. "'To your descendants, I give this land, from the river of Egypt to the great river, the river Euphrates, the land of the Kenites, the Kenizzites, the Kadmonites, the Hittites, the Perizzites, the Rephaim, the Amorites, the Canaanites, the Girgashites, and the Jebusites'" (Genesis 15:18-21). No other king expanded Israel's influence so far. In that sense, only David truly fulfilled God's promise to Abram. It was also David who conquered Jerusalem and made it the holy city—"the city of David." No other Jewish king accomplished so much, so spectacularly.

Later generations ached for the glorious times of King David, whose territorial conquests became an emblem of a great spiritual empire to a nation whose every action vibrated with spiritual content. Thus, David is a compelling model for a Messiah who will rescue Israel from the "north country" of subjugation to sin. But a sharp spiritual scalpel is needed to separate the twin notions of spiritual and territorial empire.[4]

What was the soul of David really like? He was a king of "great personal charisma," says author Jonathan Kirsch in his book, *King David*. His wonderful story, Kirsch says, "anticipates the romantic lyricism and tragic grandeur of Shakespeare, the political wile of Machiavelli, and the modern psychological insight of Freud."[5] David was "the most human character of the Bible,"[6] says historian Abram Leon Sachar. David was human all right—to the point of criminality. He is a stalker, as he lasciviously watches Bathsheba bathe. He goes on to commit adultery with her, and to make sure he can keep her, he murders her husband, Uriah, in cowardly fashion. This can hardly be the character of the Messiah who is to come.

The Messiah will have all the charisma of David and more, we are told. He will be a king who is both greater and free of taint. Like David, he will build an empire for Israel, but it will not be a territorial empire that criminally subjugates other peoples. This kingdom will be one that is pleasing to God the Father. The Gospel of Matthew ties all these threads together through the clever use of irony. At the outset, Matthew lists the twenty-eight generations that lived between King David and Jesus's father, Joseph.

Matthew then tells us that Joseph is not Jesus's real father after all. "Now the birth of Jesus the Messiah took place in this way. When his mother Mary had been engaged to Joseph, but before they lived together, she was found to be with child from the Holy Spirit" (Matthew 1:18). Matthew's irony reveals that Jesus is descended legally from David for outward purposes, which fulfills the prophecy. But he is not descended from David, blood from sinful blood. Jesus is the Son of the Most High God. His empire will embrace all kingdoms in peace, and it will endure forever, unlike David's territorial empire.

The Father Whose Name We Can Hallow

The final prophet, the Son of the Most High, the only one who has "seen" the Father, reveals God the Father in all his fullness to the Father's children. This high aristocratic Father sides with the poor, we discover. "'Blessed are the poor in spirit, for theirs is the kingdom of heaven. Blessed are those who mourn, for they will be comforted. Blessed are the meek, for they will inherit the earth'" (Matthew 5:3-5). God, the father of every royal line, is not interested in a person's status. He sides with the deprived and the unfortunate, if they will let him.

At the end of our search, we find that God the Father is not a despot who hates those who do not know him, such as the benighted Philistines and the wretched Moabites. He wants to help the ignorant. "And Jesus came and said to them, 'All authority in heaven and on earth has been given to me. Go therefore and make disciples of all nations, baptizing them in the name of the Father and of the Son and of the Holy Spirit, and teaching them to obey everything that I have commanded you'" (Matthew 28:18-20). Don't destroy the infidel with the sword, Jesus says, and do not Lord it over the spiritually uncertain. Be patient. Educate them. If you must use death as a tool of conversion, let it be your own willingness to die for the truth.

Jesus also illuminates the genocidal instructions given by the prophet Samuel to Saul, and turns them upside down. There is indeed a fiery hell awaiting any "Amalekites" who prevent people from entering the promised land of the kingdom of God. But this hell is in the afterlife and it is a hell of their own making. It is not willed upon them by God the Father.

In the twenty-first century we see the Father—as revealed by Jesus—as an ancient and a modern God. He is still the judge whose wrath the ancient Jews feared, but he cares about the natural environment just as we have learned to do—almost too late. "Are not five sparrows sold for two pennies? Yet not one of them is forgotten in God's sight. But even the hairs of your head are all counted" (Luke 12:6-7). This is a Father who cares about his children and everything around them. But the children will do better if they behave themselves.

Jesus puts forward a powerful morality, but one that cannot be put into a box as so many church martinets try to do to bolster their own power over us. Jesus warns businessmen to be ethical by condemning their ugly practices in the temple. At the same time, he returns to Caesar what is Caesar's—money. He also sets a very high sexual standard: "But I say to you that everyone who looks at a woman with lust has already committed adultery with her in his heart" (Matthew 5:28). Yet he forgives the woman taken in actual adultery. He condemns all kinds of material excess, which surely includes drunkenness, but he provides wine at the marriage feast of Cana for guests who must have been tipsy already. Finally, Jesus gives us admonitions that are pure hyperbole and leaves us to figure them out for ourselves. "If your right eye causes you to sin, tear it out and throw it away; it is better for you to lose one of your members than for the whole body to be thrown into hell" (Matthew 5:29).

The morality that flows from God the Father through Jesus is as broad as humanity itself. But it is also a counsel of perfection—nothing less:

> "If anyone strikes you on the right cheek, turn the other also; and if anyone wants to sue you and take your coat, give your cloak as well; and if anyone forces you to go one mile, go also the second mile. Give to everyone who begs from you, and do not refuse anyone who wants to borrow from you. You have heard that it was said 'You shall love your neighbor and hate your enemy.' But I say to you, Love your enemies and pray for those who persecute you, so that you may be children of your Father in heaven; for he makes his sun rise on the evil and the good, and sends rain on the righteous and on the unrighteous." Matthew 5:39-45

This astonishing warning to "love your enemies" strikes like a lightning bolt into the human soul, whether religious or not. It is a rule that is almost impossible to keep for almost all people, almost all the time. It would be easy to shrug it off as pie in the sky, except that the dying Jesus himself adheres to it, forgiving his tormentors as the ultimate act of love and peace. It's also worth noting from this passage in Matthew that those who love their enemies will become special children of God the Father. Clearly, the Father loves all humankind and is prepared to give every person a chance by making the sun shine on them and the rain fall on them every day of their lives.

This is a God for all people and all cultures and all times. If he was formerly a tribal God, we see that his tribe is the whole human race. If he was God of war, he is now God of peace. If he was the high autocrat of the Middle Ages, he is really a democrat. If he was formerly the Father of some, he is now revealed as the Father of all. This is a God who is greater than any human conception of his divinity. This is, once and for all, the God whose name we can joyfully hallow.

What Reconciles Us with the Divine?

We are all spiritual criminals, judging from the high counsels of perfection laid out by Jesus. We do not live up to what God the Father expects of us at any time. Is it enough, then, to hallow God the Father's name and start providing him with the honor he deserves? The answer has to be no, even by human logic. If a man rapes another man's daughter, it is not enough for the criminal to start speaking well of the woman's father in the barbershop (thereby "hallowing his name") or to tip his hat to the daughter with a smile when they pass on the street. This weak effort at a tribute, after the crime has been committed, takes on the character of mockery. Society holds the integrity of a woman's body sacred, and that holy principle must be honored by the criminal in the cauldron of self-sacrifice. If he is repentant, the criminal will surrender to the authorities and accept sentence. In the case of rape, this might mean jail for many years. When the sentence has been served and the criminal speaks well of the father and the violated family again, his respectful conduct starts to look like an earnest of sorrow and a declaration that the crime will never happen again.

Hallowing the name of a deeply insulted God can't be enough by itself, either. How much more does a loving God need to be atoned for the crimes of genocide, murder, theft, rape, malicious gossip, hatred, and widespread neglect of the poor that have been committed against him and his children through all the ages? Clearly, God the Father must be compensated heavily before his name can be respectfully hallowed. But who could deliver such service? Not an angel, nor an alien from the fifth moon of Jupiter, because neither would belong to the community of guilty people. The person making atonement must be a member of the nation that actually committed the crimes. But what human being could ever qualify? The whole human race itself could not make amends for these offenses because the person offended is so great. And God the Father's love for the criminals makes their crimes truly terrible. But there must be a solution. God the Father would not leave his children forever alienated.

Let us construct a theoretical being who might make amends to this selfless God. He or she must certainly be human, but any old garage mechanic or doctor won't do because the person offended is supremely perfect. The stand-in we are trying to imagine must be utterly innocent. That's because good jurisprudence declares that any sentence handed down by a court will be greater for a repeat offender. To turn that principle on its head, an innocent person will earn more merit by serving the full sentence voluntarily than any person who is actually guilty. This conciliator must also be of noble blood. That's because a senator or a duke suffers more from the sting of the lash or public mockery in the stocks than a farm laborer, because the noble person has his public reputation to lose, as well as his comfort. Therefore, if this voluntary "culprit" is high born, he will earn more for us by his sacrifice of atonement than if he were a nobody. So what do we have? This champion of humanity before a savaged God the Father must be human, an innocent, and a high aristocrat.

The Qualifications of Jesus

The title Jesus most commonly used was Son of Man, which is an allusion to a vision of Daniel's:

> I saw in the night visions, and, behold, one like the Son of man came with the clouds of heaven, and came to the Ancient of days, and they brought him near before him. And there was given him dominion, and glory, and a kingdom, that all people, nations and languages should serve him: his dominion is an everlasting dominion, which shall not pass away, and his kingdom that which shall not be destroyed. Daniel 7:13-14 KJV

Jesus conjured up the same imagery: "But from now on the Son of Man will be seated at the right hand of the power of God" (Luke 22:69). Jesus, the Son of Man, is the son; not of one man, Joseph, but of all humankind, through the Creator. He is the quintessential human being, the person who leads the human race in humanity. Jesus fits the first two qualifications for our stand-in. He is innocent of all crimes and can credibly represent the human race before the Father as a member of the offending people.

Jesus is also a nobleman because he is God himself, we are told. And his divinity was acclaimed by every category of person who ever met him: holy people and demons, friends and enemies, and God the Father himself. "Now, when all the people were baptized, and when Jesus also had been baptized and was praying, the heaven was opened and the Holy Spirit descended upon him in bodily form like a dove. And a voice came from heaven, 'You are my Son, the Beloved; with you I am well pleased'" (Luke 3: 21-22). This proclamation of Jesus's divinity was fully confirmed from below:

> As the sun was setting, all those who had any who were sick with various kinds of diseases brought them to him; and he laid his hands on each of them and cured them. Demons also came out of many, shouting: "You are the Son of God!" But he rebuked them and would not allow them to speak because they knew that he was the Messiah. Luke 4:40-41

The devout people of Israel could see this truth. "Nathanael replied, 'Rabbi, You are the Son of God. You are the King of Israel'" (John 1:49). In response to Jesus's question, "But who do you say that I am?" Simon Peter answered, "You are the Messiah, the Son of the living God" (Matthew 16:15-16).

The holiness of the Son of Man was so radiant, even his enemies recognized his spiritual power. In answer to the high priests' tricky questions, designed to incriminate him, Jesus said: "From now on, the Son of Man will be seated at the right hand of the power of God. All of them asked, 'Are you then the Son of God?' He said to them 'You say that I am'" (Luke 22:69-70). In the end, the high priests framed the man they suspected—deep within their consciousness—to be the Son of God, and they persuaded the Romans to execute him. Jesus fits all the criteria for the innocent, noble, human being who can atone for humanity's crimes before God the Father.

The Sacrifice of Jesus

The Jesus we know was many people. He was a man of peace—the "gentle Jesus meek and mild" of the nursery school. He was a source of divine wisdom that has kept the finest theologians madly theologizing for two-thousand years. He was a man of peace. And at the same time, he was a man of action—a great warrior in the most noble tradition.

During the 1982 war for the Falkland Islands between England and Argentina, Colonel H. Jones died leading the Parachute Regiment in the Battle of Goose Green. "H," as he was known, was shot by the enemy as he stormed a hill at the head of the soldiers under his command. When Jones's death was announced, a journalist asked a British officer why a commander would be in a position where he could be shot by the enemy. The officer was contemptuous of the question. "There is a tradition in the British Army," he replied tartly, "that officers lead from the front."[7] And so it is with the Son of Man, the descendant of the great warrior, King David. He, too, leads from the front.

The King's beloved army of the poor in spirit goes boiling over the ramparts of its security, eager to take on the forces of evil, which are everywhere and in all places. The wealthy stay in the rear, cocooned within their comfort, fearful of the risks outside the walls. At the head of the ragtag army of the poor is the symbol of victory—a flag with a white lamb lying on a blood red field. In the far distance, ahead of the standard, can be seen a lonely figure. It is the King himself, leading the troops. And like all good generals, he has a simple strategy. He will draw the enemy upon his royal self and so, weaken it. After all, the front line of his army is made up of the refuse of humanity—loving Southern black slaves, hospitable bone-poor peasants, "trouble-makers" in all walks of life who mouth off about "social justice" and put their families' livelihoods at risk. All of them are volunteers to the front line, and many are casualties, already maimed for life. It's unlikely they will have the strength to withstand the full onslaught of the forces of evil. They must have the support of the King.

In A.D. 33, at an execution ground called "the Skull," the soldiers have him. They stand around, gloating and laughing. They are free to commit all kinds of atrocities on his royal person. But the King is not their captive. He has submitted of his own free will, as part of his majestic strategy. Therefore, some vestige of his royal dignity must remain. He is allowed one bleak prerogative as a warrior king. "None of his bones shall be broken" (John 19:36). This is an ancient prophesy that refers to the way the Jews were to eat the Paschal lamb—without breaking any of the bones (Numbers 9:12; Psalm 34:20).

But Jesus is still made to suffer all three basic human torments in their fullest measure—pain, humiliation, and abandonment. The pain includes the sting of the lash, the hammering of a crown of thorns onto his head, and the slow agonizing suffocation of the crucifixion. Humiliation comes while he hangs nailed to the cross, stark naked, between two thieves, while his enemies jeer at his bogus aura of divinity and his naked, tortured body. Jesus is so totally and utterly humiliated by all this that he "emptied himself," in the words of Paul (Philippians 2:7). Jesus also suffers the piercing torment of watching his mother watch him die, trying hard not to sharpen his pain by shedding her tears. He also knows the wretched dismay of realizing that his closest friends believe he is a failure.

Unbroken bones may be a noble prerogative for the Lamb of God, but it is not enough to assuage the agony of the dying King, which goes on for hours. In the end, it is too much even for him. At the moment of his death, this holiest of men cries out the first line of Psalm 22: "'Eloi, Eloi, lema sabacthani?' which means, 'My God, My God, why have you forsaken me?'" (Mark 15:34). At his last, Jesus is totally abandoned at the moment of his greatest agony. Or is he? During his years of teaching, Jesus made it clear that "the Father and I are one" (John 10:30). So what do we know of God the Father, hidden away beyond space and time, as he watches the crucifixion, unwilling to reach out to his dying Son, for our sake?

Who could stand the howl of grief that must have echoed from God the Father at that moment? Fortunately for us, his cataclysmic anguish is filtered out by the thick, gross screen of the finite world. But not quite. "At that moment, the curtain of the temple was torn in two from top to bottom. The earth shook, and the rocks were split" (Matthew 27:51). And darkness covered the earth, and the dead rose up out of their graves and walked through Jerusalem. This is the turning point of the ages. In full public view, the Creator of the universe has allowed himself to be executed in disgrace, so that he can hope against hope that the people he created, and whose very life he holds in the palm of his hand, will perhaps now agree that he has earned the right to be their king.

The crucifixion is the greatest of tragedies, involving the most noble of victims. But it is not a Thomas Hardy tragedy, in which a petty malevolent Fate takes delight in twisting a good man's actions into his downfall. It is not a Greek tragedy in which a noble Destiny causes high misfortune that could not be predicted. The crucifixion is a Shakespearian tragedy, in which the downfall flows from a human character flaw. But the flaw is ours, and it brings the tragedy on the innocent Jesus.

The crucifixion is also a romance, a touchingly triumphant love story. Although Jesus suffered fear and the most excruciating pain, he never withdrew, broken, into himself. He always rejoiced in the people that God the Father had given him, both good and bad. Before he was arrested, he got down on his hands and knees and washed the dust off his friends' feet. This act of humility has been imitated by other monarchs with a solemn Holy Thursday ceremony of washing the feet of the poor. But mindful of their rulers' dignity, sycophantic courtiers allow them only to wash the already cleansed feet of carefully chosen "beggars." Jesus really washed dusty feet. This King of kings is more humble than the kings he rules.

There were other acts of love by this dying man. To his grieving mother, Jesus gives a son to take his place, so that she can be provided for. To a thief dying at his side, he promises heaven the next day. For his executioners, while they are in the very act of killing him, he enters an early plea of defense at the court of justice, even before it convenes: "Father, forgive them: for they do not know what they are doing" (Luke 23:34). The story of the death of Jesus is a romance, one of the finest love stories ever told.

The crucifixion is also high ritual, a sacred ceremony performed in public to call upon the deity. Ancient pagan priests tried to command awe in their devotees by means of mumbo jumbo, obscene masks, and other terrifying paraphernalia. The crucifixion is the most awe-inspiring ritual ever performed because it is not a hollow play or a formula relying on costume and drama. It is a vividly real act of powerful significance, performed by the deity itself in human form. If we were not inured to its ritual power by spiritual boredom and material distraction, we would be thunderstruck.

What Lies Behind Jesus's Sacrifice?

It's all very well to apply human principles of jurisprudence to Jesus's death, such as the innocence and nobility of the stand-in. But these yardsticks can hardly be used to gauge the actions of the Godhead. God the Father is a judge, but he is not a lawyer of the court. Our legal analysis leaves open many questions, particularly about the person who received Jesus's sacrifice and his response to it. But how can we penetrate the mind and motives of the divine? When Jesus himself talks about God the Father's enthusiasms, he uses the language of human emotion. God the Father "loves" us, he says. The Christian church tells us that God is "offended" by our sins and he is "pleased" with our sacrifices. These are also emotions. Deep down, emotions are movements of the spirit that manifest in the human body as laughter, tears, and long faces. God is a spirit himself, and if humans are a little like him, he must be a little like us. So perhaps we can analyze his response to the crucifixion in the language of emotion.

Is God the Father a haughty autocrat who could only be appeased for our sins by the drawn-out agony and death of his only Son? Would nothing else have assuaged his anger at our crimes? Or was he compelled to accept his Son's death with reluctance? If so, why did he accept it at all? This role of God the Father in Jesus's death is better understood if we try to figure exactly how this sacrifice works. What did Jesus actually do for the Father, or give him or save him from, by the sacrifice of his life on the cross? And how does God the Father respond?

In the most basic terms, Jesus accepted death for a noble cause. The foreknowledge of his crucifixion in the Garden of Gethsemane was so vivid it may have induced a rare medical phenomenon—hematidrosis, in which blood under great stress leaks from the capillaries into the sweat glands and then appears as red drops on the skin. Jesus could have fled from this terror, but he did not. At the same time, he did not want to embrace his death, unless it was absolutely necessary. "'My Father, if it is possible, let this cup pass from me; yet not what I want but what you want'" (Matthew 26: 39). In this way, Jesus gave his obedience to God the Father as a reluctant personal decision, one made with integrity. Jesus's willing submission compensates God the Father for our own disobedience every single day of our lives. Because Jesus is the quintessential human being, his act of humble obedience is ours, too, if we embrace it.

Jesus was executed because he would not repudiate his teaching about God the Father and the kingdom of God, all of which threatened the Jewish leaders, who wanted to make spiritual decisions for the people themselves, without interference. This is the second service Jesus performed for God the Father—to be a martyr to the truth, and that decision compensates for the lies told billions of times a day for thousands of years by humans everywhere. Jesus also earned great moral authority for God the Father, the person to whom he dedicated his martyrdom.

When the twin towers of the World Trade Center collapsed on September 11, 2001, in New York City, more than two-hundred-fifty firemen and police officers gave their lives trying to rescue the victims. Two months later, New York's mayor, Rudy Giuliani, declared that the work of cleaning up the site must progress more quickly so that it could be completed. Firefighters on the site objected, saying the ruins should still be treated with reverence as a shrine to their fallen comrades. "We never abandon our brothers, dead or alive," one of them said. The media argued that the firefighters should be heard because they had gained great moral authority by their brothers' sacrifice of life. How much more moral authority does Jesus's martyrdom gain for God the Father—in the eyes of all people of whatever religion, even if they do not believe that Jesus himself was God? This is the third service Jesus performed for God the Father, the salute of martyrdom.

Jesus's death yields even more wisdom when Scripture is consulted. Hanging on the cross, Jesus fulfills many ancient prophecies, and it seems as if all the Old Testament was written to point forward to his life and death. At the moment of the crucifixion, everything ancient falls into place, and what was opaque becomes clear. During the flight of the Israelites from Egypt, for example, the ancient priest Aaron sacrificed the lives of rams and bullocks to God for the renewal of the community's spiritual life. Gold and jewels could not be sacrificed because they were dead things that would just lie on the altar. Living animals have a spirit that can be sent directly to the Creator. In return for this giving up of wealth, or "sacrifice," God released the community from its sins. This was an unequal bargain for God the Father, who got the spirit of bullocks to balance against human insults. But it was the best the Jews could do at the time.

The Letter to the Hebrews in the New Testament explains how Jesus's sacrifice transcends Aaron's, because Jesus's life is much more sacred than livestock: "For if the blood of goats and bulls, with the sprinkling of the ashes of a heifer, sanctifies those who have been defiled so that their flesh is purified, how much more will the blood of Christ, who through the eternal spirit offered himself without blemish to God, purify our conscience from dead works to worship the loving God!" (Hebrews 9:13-14).

Jesus perfects Aaron's priesthood and rises above it by offering to God not just beasts, but his own life, once and for all. But Jesus's sacrifice goes deeper than just the sacrifice of a wonderful human being. Jesus is one person with two natures, human and divine. He is the projection of the living God into humanity, and at the same time, he is the Son of Man, whose perfect humanity is absorbed up into his divinity. He is the one person in whom God and humankind are completely united. By reconciling man and God within himself, Jesus accomplishes what any priest tries to do at any religious service—the reconciliation of the human community with God the Father. But Jesus is more than just any old priest at a Sunday service. He is the High Priest in the very heart of his divine and human self. He accomplishes reconciliation, not time after time through a series of church rituals, but once and forever, because he is eternally God as well as forever man, always reconciled.

The sacrifice of Jesus the High Priest goes in two directions—from humanity to God the Father, and from God the Father to humanity. God the Father sacrifices to humanity his only son Jesus as a king, a teacher, a healer, and a martyr. Jesus gives back to God the Father the life of the Son of Man, which is the heart and soul of humankind. He does this in a most noble way. He does not commit ritual hara-kiri on an altar. He accepts execution, but only because if he were to continue to remain alive he would have to betray the Father's truth. And he makes this sacrifice on our behalf. Insofar as each individual wishes it, the whole of humankind takes part in the Son of Man's sacrifice to the truth, as a free gift. All truly repentant criminals are born again by Jesus's act. Even the worst crimes of the foulest psychopath and the most prolific pedophile are forgiven and forgotten, at no cost but the price of the criminal accepting the Son of God's sacrifice with a whole heart and humbly surrendering to the community.

But what of God the Father? The question arises again: Did his high conceit call for the sacrifice of his only Son before he would bend down from his great height to forgive his race of servants? After all, God the Father can do whatever he likes, including forgive anybody for anything, without conditions. So why does it have to be his Son's horrible death that works the trick? The answer that we give to this question always reflects the character of the God we think we know, in the age in which we give the answer.

In medieval times, the belief was that we are all wretches before the purity and majesty of almighty God, who rules from the top down. Such a great God can only be appeased by a great sacrifice, it was thought, something that no ordinary human could ever accomplish. That's why it must be the death of God's Son. But that view is outdated, because it is based on an antique vision of a prideful God the Father.

The truth is more subtle. God the Father accepted the sacrifice of his own Son as atonement for our crimes because of the weakness in our human nature, not the magnificence in his own. If the Father merely forgave all our sins with a wave of his hand, his forgiveness would appear to be sentimental. His flippant pardons would make light of our crimes by their ease and arbitrariness. We might expect to be airily forgiven all over again every time we offended. And we would have little incentive to reform, which is always a hard thing to do. On the other hand, if we had to do penance ourselves for all our crimes—directly to God the Father—we would rightly believe that there's not much we can do to properly make amends. And we would slip into despair.

What earns our forgiveness more convincingly is the sacrifice of the Son of God, something far more terrible than any sentence we could ever serve ourselves. This awesome sacrifice of God to God convinces us that God's forgiveness of such crimes as murder, rape, and slander is concrete and binding on him and on us, because it is earned at such a high price. In these terms, our rescue becomes more compelling to our own sense of justice. And for those who can grasp the gravity of Jesus's sacrifice, it can only prompt real reform in response to his generosity.

Finally, what of the compact between Father and Son as Jesus lay dying on the cross, and the Father stood his distance, probably grieving? Jesus's sacrifice was not a surprise to God the Father, because the Father knows everything, and in any case, Jesus and the Father are said to be one. Perhaps we can say that Jesus's death on the cross was the culmination of a conspiracy between Father and Son in the high halls of eternity to rescue humankind at a terrible cost to both of them. The Father's consent to the crucifixion is not the action of some high autocrat. His consent, and his grief, both flow from the anxiety of a loving Father for both his Son and his sons and daughters.

The Celestial Joke

The crucifixion is a living ritual, a high tragedy, and a love story. It is also a huge joke. In fact, it is a piece of humor so divine as to be almost incomprehensible to the human mind from within its tragic setting. But it is humor nevertheless. Humor is an insight into the dual nature of human beings—creatures who reach for the stars and fall flat on their faces, persons made in the image of the infinite God, out of mud. We can imagine a cantankerous recluse, who rushes out of his house to castigate the children playing noisily in the street. He slips on a banana skin and falls, thud, on his bottom. The whole street bursts into laughter. The recluse relents, and the children resume their play. All humor is like this—a warm embrace of failure, a flash of understanding into the breadth and illogic of our nature, a surge of something that prevents humankind from taking itself too seriously. And so it is with the crucifixion.

The council of elders of the Jews chooses a dark humorless policy of manipulating the Romans into murdering Jesus to preserve the elders' social advantage. Jesus accepts execution and turns it to the redemption of all penitent people, including his own murderers, if they want it. The evil conduct of the human race is permitted by God the Father, but it is also turned on its head by the crucifixion of Jesus and forgotten, if only the children will be happy with him. In the secret places of infinity, the laughter of the Almighty and his Son rings down the ages at the memory of how they turned the tables on humankind, and changed would-be monsters into loveable fools. The black, lonely, torment of the dying Jesus forever sweetens the laughter of God the Father's children, by liberating them forever from their evil work. The crucifixion is a gift of humor all the more precious because it is so costly to the humorist.

How Are We to Say "Hallowed Be Thy Name"?

We now have all the ingredients that will enable us to hallow God's name well. We have a good idea of the Father's character, at least insofar as it has been revealed to us. We also know that we can hallow God's name by embracing Jesus's sacrifice as the divine act that rescues us from our criminal conduct. And we have some understanding of the crucifixion—at least so we think.

We also know from Jesus's prayer that we cannot hallow God the Father's name by ourselves, even after the crucifixion has liberated us to do so. That's why we do not pray "Father, we will hallow your name from now on." What we pray with humility is this: "Father, may your name be hallowed amongst us"—in other words, "Please inspire all the peoples of the world, by your grace, to pay reverence to your holiness, and bring about reconciliation with you."

The word *hallowed* means "to honor as holy," according to the Oxford English Dictionary. The same dictionary says *holy* means "perfect and to be revered," or "belonging to God." What this all means is that God's "holiness" is the dynamic power of his goodness. To "hallow" God's "name" is to celebrate his character as being powerfully good, and to recognize that God's character brings wholeness to everything it touches.

When we pray "Father, hallowed be thy name," we start heading toward the high goal of the coming of the kingdom, which is sought in the next petition, "Thy kingdom come." The first transformation of the spirit along this road to the kingdom is a cleansing, like taking a shower. We wash out all the soiled passions that remain after we say "Father," such as anxiety, greed, envy, and the miasma of stress we live through without ever fully understanding why. These spiritual toxins force us to desecrate God's holy gifts or his sacred people for our own selfish and materialistic purposes. We argue and we fight and we gossip about others, sometimes without even intending to do so. But this base conduct of the spirit flees before the inner purification of "Hallowed be thy name." And we pray that all people in the world will enjoy the same liberation.

The next steps on the road to the kingdom are constructive. As we hallow God's name with greater sincerity, we recognize that all that God creates is sacred. With newly opened eyes and a free soul, we see the brilliant beauty of the birds and the flowers and the rats and the cockroaches in all their fullness, because these creatures were made by God the Father and have a holy purpose. We consume the resources that God the Father has placed before us, but we do so now with a new gratitude and a concern that these gifts only be used for the most serious of purposes—our nourishment and our protection. Waste of anything at all becomes a crime. And we pray that all people will practice the same reverence.

But God's creation is more than honey badgers and bumble bees and coal. It is also the greatest of his masterpieces: humankind. When we said "Father," we embraced all others as our brothers and sisters. Now by saying "Hallowed be thy name," we hold as sacred the special local character that distinguishes Berbers from Bushmen, Muslims from Macedonians, Americans from Tamils. We discern all the cultural differences among God's peoples with joy and a sense of wonder, and we celebrate the sacred qualities of the whole of humankind in all its diversity. And we pray that others' eyes will be opened in the same way.

Hallowing God's name helps us to rise above our crass animal urges in favor of being more fully human, in every sense. We take no further interest in pride, which is a form of base animal competition and in the end, hollow. We lose our animal instinct to cower before strength or bow before the assaults of domineering people—the kind of flight impulse that causes a stag to back away when threatened by a bigger stag. In front of bullies, we no longer suffer the pain of being dominated. We are free to see bullying for what it is, and we are still free to love the bully. When we hallow the Father's name, fame becomes irrelevant because it is a sterile plant we cultivate in a garden planted for ourselves alone, instead of our looking over the fence at the endless panorama of God the Father's country, populated by his beautiful people. In every imaginable way, hallowing God's name elevates us above our baser nature into a fuller humanity.

The process of hallowing God's name is like courtship. A lover might say about his beloved, "I worship the very ground she walks on." And when he marries her and lives with her, he and she come to look and behave alike because they imitate the one they love and come to look on the world through the same eyes. When God's name is held holy, a similar metamorphosis occurs. A person's outlook is lightened until every thing and every person becomes beautiful and the person becomes holy himself and more like God, the Holy One. And we pray that all the people of the world will be so transformed.

But hallowing God's name is not just a formula of words or a wholesome internal psychology. "Father, hallowed be thy name" calls for deeds, even politics. It calls upon us to happily distribute our talents to all God the Father's children without favor, and to recognize and share their gifts without a hierarchy of values. It calls on us to support the poor and liberate those of God the Father's children who are oppressed. It calls us to do concrete good for as many people as we can, everywhere we can, because they are all holy.

"Father, Hallowed be thy name" is another step forward in the great adventure of Jesus's prayer. It calls on all our energy and all our humanity, just like the adventure of climbing Mount Everest. But hallowing God's name climbs a mountain that is higher than any in the Himalayas. It calls for a direct frontal assault on the mountain of the self. We may reach the higher levels of this lofty pinnacle and look out over beautiful vistas of the world and the spirit, but we are unlikely to ever reach the top. Hallowing God's name is an adventure for a lifetime. One that never comes to an end.

4

Thy Kingdom Come

At its heart, what Jesus taught the disciples is a prayer for the coming of the kingdom. "Thy kingdom come" is not only the midpoint, it is the prayer's focus and the principal objective of Christianity itself. The rest of the prayer buttresses this petition, in the way that foothills support a mountain on either side. We must pray the whole of Jesus's prayer, rather than just "Thy kingdom come," because we are never ready for the kingdom's coming. We are spiritually illiterate, greedy for material things, vengeful, and worried about problems that don't matter at all. We must say the whole prayer, again and again, to prepare for the kingdom's coming—which is secretly our greatest desire, if we but knew it. But the kingdom's coming is inevitable, because that is the destiny of humankind, the beloved children of God.

The other five petitions in the prayer lead up to, and keep us in the shadow of the coming of this high kingdom. "Father" opens an awareness of God as progenitor of all. Without this intelligence, there can be no coming of the King. "Hallowed be thy name" prays for reconciliation of the nation and this Father-King. When harmony is achieved (though it never is), the world is ready to enter into unity with God the King. "Thy kingdom come."

The prayer's second half begs for the faith we need on the journey to the coming kingdom. We pray for daily sustenance ("bread") so that we won't worry about where the next sandwich is coming from. We ask for forgiveness so that we won't twist our guts with remorse and lose sight of where we are going. And we ask for holy leadership in our upward quest— "And lead us not into temptation."

The search for the kingdom goes on all the time, in all places. Each decent person seeks it in his or her own way, with his or her own talents. But all seek the same thing in one of its million manifestations, which are all one kingdom. Some come close to finding what they seek but stop short. Others turn away to the easy comfort of baser amusements. Some never understand what they are looking for and search aimlessly. And so it is all over the world. The kingdom is coming in one place and going in another. It comes where it was going, and it goes where it was coming. But the prayer is clear. We don't say: "Establish your kingdom here and now, we beg you." We say "Thy kingdom come," which is mysterious in its anticipated fulfillment. The kingdom comes—in word and in deed—but mostly it is yet to come. We await the final coming, the sunset of the world, when the sheep are parted from the goats.

Why Is God's Realm Called a Kingdom?

Why does God wish his people to live under the reign of a king, when that kind of rule is discredited and buried deep in the dust of the ages? History contains too many kings and queens who were arrogant or depraved or surrounded with toadies who lorded it over the people. "Power tends to corrupt, and absolute power corrupts absolutely," as Lord Acton of Aldenham put it in the late nineteenth century. "Great men are almost always bad men," he added.[1] And this principle applied most commonly to kings. Now, most kingdoms have been swept into the rubbish bin of history. The few that remain in places like England and the Netherlands have been reduced to ceremonial offices that preserve colorful pageantry and a sense of history.

Nowadays, we want to live in a state that is not at the mercy of a supreme ruler's whims, but that guarantees the state's ideals in a constitution. The noble slogans ring clear: "Life, Liberty, and the Pursuit of Happiness." "Peace, Order, and Good Government." With our rights written in stone, we feel safe from governmental abuse. So why does Jesus insist on talking about God as King?

The answer is that all kingdoms—from the Pharaohs' Egypt to Henry VIII's England—are a crude, corruptible model of what Jesus is talking about: the rule of God in the world. For that reason, an earthly king is, in theory, the perfect ruler, because he is a reflection of the divine ruler, albeit in a cracked and tarnished mirror. An earthly king possesses everything he needs to rule the people wisely. He has the power and, supposedly, the wisdom. He has no fear of offending public opinion, because he is on the throne for life. He is never partisan: he can consult the finest advisers of every stripe, but he is not obliged to follow any of their counsel. A king can help the poor and shrug off complaints from the rich. A king can ensure social justice, because he is not a legal code, which oppresses some citizens by its mechanical nature. A king is a living person who can deal justly with the disorder of humanity and make fair exceptions to fair laws. A king is the best of all possible rulers—potentially.

In modern times, we prefer to vote the government in or out, according to its performance. But an elected government may not be able to do what is best for the country, because it must court the voters, even when they are driven to make the wrong demands by a frenzy whipped up by the media. According to one delegate to the U.S. Constitutional Convention in Philadelphia in 1787: "The people immediately should have as little to do as may be about the government. They lack information and are constantly liable to be misled."[2] But another problem is that democratically elected political leaders must kowtow to wealthy people who can fund their election campaigns. All in all, democracy is "the worst form of Government, except for all those other forms that have been tried from time to time," as Sir Winston Churchill put it.[3]

A king is the finest of rulers because he is anointed by God. At least, that's what ancient peoples were told. This canon was reinforced by coronation of the king at the hands of the top spiritual leader. A few monarchs even claimed they were gods themselves and assumed powers of life and death over their subjects.

If the king is God's anointed, he must be the finest person in the nation. Otherwise, God would not have chosen him. That's why the king stands for the most noble humanity. He is virtuous, courageous, and merciful. He is the true "son" of the people, which means he is the sacred symbol of the ordinary person as hero. Even Mao Tse-Tung, the Communist emperor of China, assumed the title "Son of the Masses" to suggest he was the embodiment of all the Chinese people's finest aspirations.

The ideal king's heroism is a beacon to all decent people who try to live by a set of ideals, which they fail to reach, with sorrow. For these good people, the king is living proof that their moral ambitions are attainable, even though they themselves may fail. But the king does not dwell above his subjects. He is their comfort. In the ideal kingdom, every person loves the nation through another person—the king—rather than through any cold institution, such as a republic. This love of the king is the core of the state, because it is not one love, but two: a love of the king as a heroic person, and a love of the king as the embodiment of the beloved country. And these two loves are fused into one indivisible enthusiasm.

This sacred compact between king and people was well understood in ancient times. In 480 B.C., a squadron of three hundred Spartans held the mountain pass at Thermopylae against two million soldiers of the Persian Empire—a battle ratio of about seven thousand to one. The Spartans were led by their king, Leonidas, who felt it was his duty to stand at the head of his army on its heroic mission to save Greece, rather than sit safely in his palace and receive dispatches. The king was one of the first to die, along with many of his nobles, because he was in the front line. According to Herodotus, as the remaining Spartans broke their weapons on the endless waves of oncoming Persians, they continued to fight on with their nails and teeth until they were all killed and their bodies were desecrated by the enraged enemy. An ancient inscription at the site read: "Go tell the Spartans, Stranger passing by, that here, obedient to their laws, we lie."[4]

The notion that the king is subsumed into the soul of the nation continues into modern times. During World War II, Queen Elizabeth of England, who later became the Queen Mother, was asked why the royal children were not evacuated from Buckingham Palace in the heart of heavily bombed London. She replied: "The children could not go without me. I won't leave the king. And the king will never leave." King George VI felt it was his duty to remain with his people as their living banner. When a bomb fell on Buckingham Palace, Queen Elizabeth was heard to exclaim: "Oh, thank God! Now we have something in common with the people of Battersea."[5]

The British people reciprocated this appreciation of the king's heroic role. In November 1940, a lightly armed British merchant vessel called *Jervis Bay* was guarding a transatlantic convoy of food heading for besieged England. When a German battleship, *Admiral Scheer,* threatened the convoy, *Jervis Bay* attacked it to give the convoy time to scatter. *Jervis Bay*'s captain, E. S. Fogarty Fegen, reported this suicidal action to the British

Admiralty by radio. He most likely ended his signal with: "God save the king." In other words, "We may not survive this action, but we pray that Almighty God will preserve the life of Britain as it is embodied in the person of His Majesty." *Jervis Bay* was sunk and the captain and much of the crew were lost. The British government honored them for their "devotion."[6]

In a kingdom, the people love the king, love the nation through the king, and love each of their neighbors through this love of the nation and the king. A kingdom fosters the joy and happiness of all the people, because the king's subjects have a luminous person to follow rather than an arid duty to a legal structure. The ideal kingdom is the rule of love—a love that binds the king and the nation and the individual in complete unity.

The Divine Kingdom

In God's kingdom, the King is much more than a perfect earthly king. He is the womb of the nation, because he created each of his subjects out of nothing. He is the judge who decides who will enter the kingdom and who will remain outside gnashing their teeth. He is the people's final destination, because the kingdom is the unity—at last—of God the Father's children with the King. Within the kingdom, the King enters into communion with each of his subjects, fully and finally. The more they love him, the more they become united with him, in the most mysterious ways. But the King's embrace does not eclipse their identity. Each person is subsumed into the King and liberated into the greater fullness of his or her humanity. Outside the kingdom, there is only a diminished life.

Jesus unveiled this mysterious union of human and God in the kingdom by saying:

> "I ask not only on behalf of these, but also on behalf of those who will believe in me through their word, that they may all be one. As you Father are in me and I am in you, may they also be in us, so that the world may believe that you have sent me. The glory that you have given me I have given them, so that they may be one, as we are one, I in them and you in me, that they may become completely one, so that the world may know that you have sent me and have loved them, even as you have loved me." John 17:20-23

The kingdom of God is the full, holy, and ecstatic communion of the nation of the world—and each individual—with God the Father, the High Priest, and the King.

The kingdom of God is a dictatorship—what else can it be?—yet at the same time it is democratic, which is one of its more delightful paradoxes. The kingdom is autarkic, because there is no authority greater than God's, and no person can reasonably challenge that authority (although many try). The kingdom is democratic, because this all-powerful king is called to the throne and kept there by popular demand. He is too humble to impose himself on his people. That's why the coming of the kingdom must be requested: "Thy kingdom come." It is foolish, though, to think it is the people's asking that will bring the king. He comes by his own majesty, according to his own timetable. His coming is by his will and by the uncoerced will of his subjects.

The key to this mystery is God's action within us. God the Father inspires everybody to get down on their knees and pray. But he does this invisibly. His techniques range from the advice of a holy person to a brilliant sunset to the sharp sting of misfortune. God has no choice but to use slaps of pain because some people only think about him when they face death or when their children are in trouble. The response to God's barely heard whisper varies in as many ways as there are human beings to hear it. Some dismiss the divine voice out of hand. They go after more wealth to ease the pain, or drown out the chanting of the priests, or nurse a satisfying hatred, or complain about those weird neighbors next door—all of which seems comforting at the time. Others take the hint and squirm, but defer the work of praying until later. Many do start to pray. And once a prayer is said, the game of selfishness is lost. Prayer allows God the Father, who is always knocking on the door, to enter a person's heart, where he can inspire that person to take two steps forward and seek the kingdom.

The Kingdom's Gates Are Opened

The kingdom of God is democratic because the King works harder than any earthly politician to get elected. In fact, he suffers all kinds of humiliations and atrocities, just to bring his subjects into the kingdom. He drags along behind some people for years like a dog, hoping to be thrown a little goodwill. He hangs around back alleys, hoping to catch the notice of pimps and prostitutes to bring them into the kingdom. One Spanish order of nuns does precisely that kind of work on his behalf. Jesus, too, preferred the company of sinners, with the same humble ambition.

The King approaches us from every direction, hopefully. He comes to us from below as a social outcast and a failure, under the hammer of the executioner—a figure of sorrow, suffocating to death on the cross, one whom we should ache to comfort and love. He comes to us from above in the glory of the conquest of death, a concept too brilliant and too noble for the human mind to entertain, if it had not happened. He approaches his people any way he feels might prove effective. He is a hardworking king—and a humble king—because he makes sure every aspect of the kingdom is chosen freely. The kingdom's democratic character even extends to the most amazing truth in the history of the world—the resurrection. This great wonder is not forced down our throats. It is only embraced in trust, individually and freely.

The resurrection is God's imperial conquest of death, the moment of his great triumph on Earth, and the clearest signpost on the high road to his kingdom. But it is only a quiet invitation to believe, not a compulsion of overwhelming force, as one would expect:

> Then the disciples returned to their homes. But Mary stood weeping outside the tomb. As she wept, she bent over to look into the tomb; and she saw two angels in white sitting where the body of Jesus had been lying, one at the head, and the other at the feet. They said to her, "Woman, why are you weeping?" She said to them, "They have taken away my Lord, and I do not know where they have laid him." When she had said this she turned around and saw Jesus standing there, but she did not know that it was Jesus. Jesus said to her, "Woman why are you weeping? Whom are you looking for?" Supposing him to be the gardener, she said to him, "Sir, if you have carried him away, tell me where you have laid him, and I will take him away." Jesus said to her, "Mary." John 20:10-16

A moment of love, rather than dazzling glory.

By rising from the dead, the Son of Man reveals God's disdain for the coils of matter, an almost flippant demonstration of his divine power. The natural expectation of our prideful nature is that Jesus would emerge from the tomb more brilliant than the noonday sun, and in this moment of triumph, command belief from the most cynical of people to compensate for his humiliation on the cross. But we underestimate his sublime majesty. The risen Jesus presents himself only to his friends, and then shyly. This Son of the Most High God masters death by rising from the tomb and appearing—as a workman. This fact is almost as astonishing as the conquest of death itself. In this meek way, Jesus proves that although God is the king of beggars and bakers, princes and prostitutes, he is never, ever, a conqueror. Recognition of God's majesty, even in the magnificence of the resurrection, is always optional.

God reveals his greatest secret only to his friends. That's why the evidence of the resurrection can be dismissed by those who wish to do so. We are only told that the risen Jesus appeared to many people after his death. On one occasion, he was seen on the lakeshore cooking fish for his disciples as they came off the water from the night's fishing.

> Jesus said to them, "Come and have breakfast." Now, none of the disciples dared to ask him "Who are you?" because they knew it was the Lord. Jesus came and took the bread and gave it to them and did the same with the fish. This was now the third time that Jesus appeared to the disciples after he was raised from the dead. John 21:12-14

On another occasion, Jesus let the apostle Thomas place his hand in Jesus's side to feel the lance wound. "Although the doors were shut, Jesus came and stood among them and said 'Peace be with you.' Then he said to Thomas 'Put your finger here and see my hands. Reach out your hand and put it in my side. Do not doubt, but believe'" (John 20:26-27).

According to some, these apparitions were just the morbid hallucinations of Jesus's disciples, who were terrified by the death of their leader. Yet a ghost cannot be touched, and an apparition does not cook fish and serve it on a platter for a person to eat. The apostles were not demented either, nor fearful, because they went on bravely to spread their belief in the risen Jesus around the globe. Terrified screwballs are not capable of powerful missionary work.

But the evidence that the disciples saw and touched the biological Jesus is in no sense proof. There are still loopholes that could be exploited by any prosecution in a court of law. Are the accounts of the disciples' experiences true? Were the disciples victims of a clever hoax by those who wanted to discredit Christianity with over-the-top fantasies? Or, was there a conspiracy to "sell" Jesus by the early Christians, who invented this resurrection myth to gain proselytes? A person who wishes to do so can always find a way to reject the evidence of the resurrection. And without the resurrection, Christianity is no better than a hundred other religions that have been led by holy men. Christianity is even less, because of this outrageous, seemingly false claim of a rising from the dead. As Paul put it: "If Christ has not been raised, then our proclamation has been in vain, and your faith has been in vain" (1 Corinthians 15:14). If the resurrection is a lie, Christianity should be extirpated from Western consciousness as a fraud. Tolerance is a very weak response to such a monstrous lie, if indeed it is a lie.

The search for the coming of the kingdom requires a powerful faith, because that is a stronger link to the Godhead than a grudging acceptance of undeniable evidence. Faith involves trust, which honors the dignity of the person trusted. Faith is a relationship in love. Its opposite, the acceptance of scientific proof, involves nothing of the heart. And it gives nothing to the person "buying" the evidence, except perhaps resentment over being turned out of his comfortable intellectual home. That's why proof of the resurrection would be deadening to the spiritual life. It would be so much more lifeless science, which already infests our lives with its colossal quantities of useless data. What we need is what we are given, an invitation to faith. For this reason, the resurrection contains a delicious paradox. The risen Jesus is a person of such grace and nobility that he will not impose himself in all his glory on just anybody at all. He waits for his friends to recognize and embrace him. But his humility is precisely what makes it easy for the cynical to dismiss the resurrection as a lie, because it is not proven beyond a reasonable doubt.

The refusal of the risen Jesus to coerce—a mark of his resplendent humility—fills his story with mystery and light and the potential for a beautiful faith. The resurrection is Jesus's secret credentials, presented confidentially to an underground nation of believers.

A Taste of True Reality

But still, what is the resurrection? It is a magnificent starburst of illumination of the kingdom of God in the night of our ignorance, as if the kingdom was laid out like a map for all to see, just for a flash. The resurrection is a rent in the cosmos that allows us to peep through at the glory of the divine for just one moment in time. No, that's not quite right. In the resurrection, we are not looking at something divine, far away in infinity. The resurrection is an explosion of divinity wholly within the fabric of time and space. No, that's not right, either. Explosions create chaos. The resurrection is a vivid glimpse, in a flash, of another world that lies wholly within the world in which we live. The resurrection is a taste of true reality at its very core.

That reality is the kingdom of God, which lies at the heart of everything. The resurrection tells us that the kingdom of God is more powerful and more lasting than the mighty Roman Empire that put Jesus to death. The resurrection tells us that the kingdom of God is far greater than the tyranny of the high priests who conspired so evilly against Jesus, despite the wishes of the people. The resurrection tells us that the kingdom of God is more powerful than any other power anywhere, whether it be the myriad retinues of an Eastern potentate or a baneful cabal of office managers. The resurrection tells us that the kingdom of God will come in the face of any tyranny, no matter how apparently total.

The resurrection makes the kingdom of God universal and elevates Jesus's death on the cross in Jerusalem to a sacrifice that is efficacious for all people at all times. If Jesus had been bludgeoned to death by the pagans of ancient Britain, his martyrdom would have had little significance, because the ancient Britons were too primitive to understand what they would have done. Jesus's murder at their hands in the dank northern forests would have been of as little value as if he had been killed by a runaway train today. Instead, Jesus died in the midst of the most spiritually noble people of his time—the ancient Jews, the chosen people of God, that heroic nation that preserved God's name against the blasphemous depredations of his enemies. Alone among the ancient peoples, the Jews knew who God was and treasured that knowledge most sacredly. The crucifixion of the Son of Man in the midst of this spiritually exalted people takes on the quality of a most poignant spiritual tragedy. But while the crucifixion is indeed tragic, the resurrection takes it further.

If Jesus had stayed dead in the tomb, his sacrifice would have been a local event, momentous for only one tribe of people at a particular time. It would have been a reason for them to look inward and examine why their ancestors "shed the blood of the prophets" (Matthew 23:30). By his death on the cross, Jesus would have departed forever from his people and there would be nothing more to tell, except regrets.

Jesus's return to life elevates his death to supranational significance. He was crucified as a normal man, a Jew. He rose again in a glorified state of humanity, one that cannot be labeled as genetically Jewish or Turkish or British, but can only be construed as the splendid humanity of the entire world. The resurrection also turns Jesus's death into a free gift, an absolutely voluntary sacrifice under his own control, because the resurrection reveals that he was always beyond the power of his executioners.

It's like a person taking a holiday in Aruba. His stay is deliberate and he leaves again, whereas a person who lives in Aruba has not chosen Aruba and may be too poor to depart. And so it is with the crucifixion. We all live in the Aruba of this life and must die in it. The resurrection reveals that Jesus is the timeless one. The life and death, within time, of this timeless one can only be seen as a willing journey with purpose into the ravages of the finite, ravages that are universal to all humanity. It is the purpose of this visit of the timeless one—and his spectacular departure—that engages our fascination.

The resurrection tells us that the kingdom of God is more powerful than money—the cash that bought Judas' betrayal. The resurrection tells us that the kingdom of God is more powerful than any pain or hardship, on the cross or anywhere else. All the agony Jesus endured is conquered by his rising. The kingdom of God will also conquer all pain and all sorrow and all grieving in all of us. The resurrection tells us that the kingdom of God is more powerful than science, which talks so authoritatively about life and death, the circulation of the blood, and the tyranny of time on the human body. The resurrection reveals that the kingdom of God is more powerful than death itself, the final scientific fact. The resurrection tells us that the story of Adam and Eve can be stood on its head. We are not fallen forever from paradise, it declares. We are heading for paradise, if we want it, because there are no restraints whatsoever on the coming of the kingdom of God, if we choose it. It is coming now and in the future, and no power on Earth can ever prevent it.

The resurrection tells us that the kingdom of God lies at the very core of the reality we think we understand. It lies beyond the inanimate forces of nature, beyond science, even beyond space and time, but within them all, because that is where the King dwells and there, too, must be the kingdom. And one day we will come to understand some of this stuff, as we continue to search for the coming of the kingdom we barely understand. The crucifixion and the resurrection are the opening of the massive, creaking, hitherto impenetrable gates that lead into the secret citadel, the personal compound of the King.

Who Is the King?

Jesus's prayer points to three divine persons—the Father, the High Priest, and the King. These seem to match the three persons of the Trinity—the

Father, the Son, and the Holy Spirit. The Father, in both cases, is the origin of everything. The second person in the Trinity is the Son of God the Father, who is Jesus. In the prayer, the second person is the High Priest, who again is Jesus, because he reconciles us with the Father as he dies on the cross. The third person in the prayer, the King, would appear to be the Holy Spirit, the mysterious third person in the Trinity.

But the roles of these three persons are not clear cut. The gospels mark Jesus, not the Holy Spirit, as the descendant of King David. The angel Gabriel confirmed this to Mary: "He will be great and will be called the Son of the Most High, and the Lord God will give to him the throne of his ancestor David, He will reign over the house of Jacob forever, and of his kingdom there will be no end" (Luke 1:32-33). But the Gospel of John is more ambiguous:

> "My kingdom is not from this world," Jesus tells Pontius Pilate. "If my kingdom were from this world, my followers would be fighting to keep me from being handed over to the Jews. But as it is, my kingdom is not from here." Pilate asked him, "So you are a king?" Jesus answered, "You say that I am a king. For this I was born, and for this I came into the world, to testify to the truth. Everyone who belongs to the truth listens to my voice." John 18:36-37

Jesus is saying here that he can be considered a spiritual king, but he is really a teacher, or a prophet, who reveals the truth.

Jesus declared in one gospel passage that at the end time, when he "comes in his glory and all the angels with him," he will separate the good from the bad—the "sheep" from the "goats," and send the goats to the eternal fire (Matthew 25:31-46). But in the more spiritually penetrating Gospel of John, Jesus says his high purpose is not to decide who should enter the kingdom and who will stay out. He comes to open the kingdom's doors.

> Then Jesus cried aloud: "Whoever believes in me believes not in me but in him who sent me. And whoever sees me sees him who sent me. I have come as light into the world, so that everyone who believes in me should not remain in the darkness. I do not judge anyone who hears my words and does not keep them, for I came not to judge the world but to save the world." John 12:44-47

In any nation, it is the king's prerogative to judge who shall be exiled from the kingdom or who shall be allowed to enter. In this passage, Jesus says he is the High Priest who "saves the world" and reconciles it with God the Father, thereby opening the kingdom's doors.

The King must be the Holy Spirit, the one who appears after the kingdom's gates have been unlocked. And Jesus himself suggests this identification. "But when the Comforter is come, whom I will send unto you from the Father, even the Spirit of truth, which proceedeth from the Father, he shall testify of me" (John 15:26, KJV). And it is the Holy Spirit (of truth) that remains forever with the church that Jesus founded, and "forever" is where the kingdom comes.

The kingdom of God is a gift in love. It comes from the King himself, the Holy Spirit, and it comes directly to each person individually in baptism. "Jesus answered, 'Very truly, I tell you, no one can enter the kingdom of God without being born of water and Spirit'" (John 3:5). It's the Holy Spirit who guides the people through the opened gate of the kingdom, surely as the King. And he is the King who will rule forever over the eternal kingdom. At least, that is one interpretation of these many, complex passages. But in the final analysis it's impossible to squeeze the three infinite persons of the Trinity into these allegorical earthly roles of Father and King. And if the identity of the King is hard to pin down, his realm is even more mysterious.

The Secrets of the Kingdom of God

The kingdom of God is too sublime and too vast for our intellects to grasp. But Jesus gave us 127 pointers to its geography and its divine politics. These clues are found in 25 parables, as well as in many maxims, aphorisms, and sayings. Jesus began many of these spiritual tidbits with "Amen, I say unto you," meaning "This is most true," to underline the solemnity of what he was about to say. The parables are simple stories. They tell of common things—a mustard tree, a farmer who sows seeds, a fisherman, and birds. But they do not talk down to the listeners. Their childishly simple imagery hides the most profound truths. And like all high literature, the parables are provocative rather than exhaustive. They lay out the kingdom in colorful ways without burdening the listener with too much ratiocination or theology. The parables are always understandable, and yet—not quite. It's like looking at a ship in the harbor through a fog. "Ah! There it is. No, perhaps not! The fog has closed in again. No, wait a minute! Isn't that it over there?"

In A.D. 30, these simple tales did not reveal much to Jesus's audience. He had to explain them, even to his followers.

> Then the disciples came and asked him, "Why do you speak to them in parables?" He answered, "To you it has been given to know the secrets of the kingdom of heaven, but to them it has not been given. For to those who have, more will be given, and they will have an abundance; but from those who have nothing, even what they have will be taken away."
> Matthew 13:10-12

Here, Jesus alludes to the timeless truth that a wealthy man makes money because he owns money, and the returns on his investments pile up with compounding interest without the rich man doing much about it. And so it is with the spiritually wealthy—those who seek the kingdom. Their spiritual wealth, too, will multiply.

God's kingdom is a great fortune, one that is worth far more than any other riches a person may own. "The kingdom of heaven is like treasure hidden in a field, which someone found and hid; then in his joy he goes and sells all that he has and buys that field. Again, the kingdom of heaven is like a merchant in search of fine pearls; on finding one pearl of great value, he went and sold all that he had and bought it" (Matthew 13:44-46).

In likening the kingdom to secret riches, Jesus contrasts two lifestyles—the mundane life of ordinary people, and the exalted life of the kingdom. Where's the harm, we might ask, in writing an annual report that's true and complete but veils from the investors, within tiny footnotes, all the damaging information about the financial health of the corporation that pays the writer's wages? Isn't that corporate loyalty, after all? Surely, it's up to the shareholder to be diligent and figure it all out. Then again, isn't it wise to take out gobs of insurance on our lives and on every piece of property we own to ensure our family's financial safety? And can anybody really criticize us for taking a gourmet meal with wine after work to drain away the day's stress, or for spending two weeks a year on vacation in Marbella? Who could condemn somebody for living such a life?

And then there's this treasure hidden in a field. The treasure is so fabulous a person must strip himself to the bone for it. "If your hand causes you to stumble, cut it off... And if your eye causes you to stumble, tear it out; it is better for you to enter the kingdom of God with one eye than to have two eyes and to be thrown into hell, where the worm never dies, and the fire is never quenched" (Mark 9:43-48).

Absolutely nothing we own is more important than the kingdom of God. Even good health is not worth preserving at the cost of losing the kingdom. And when a person does work for the kingdom of God, his whole life is lightened. "The kingdom of heaven is like yeast that a woman took and mixed in with three measures of flour, until all of it was leavened" (Matthew 13:33). And the more a person sacrifices for the kingdom, the greater the reward—exponentially. "And he said to them 'Truly I tell you, there is no one who has left house or wife or brothers or parents or children, for the sake of the kingdom of God, who will not get back very much more in this age, and in the age to come eternal life'" (Luke 18:28-30).

The search for the kingdom of God is childishly simple and mysterious and bold and impossibly profound. And through our search for it in fields, in business offices, in shops and garages, and in all our everyday dealings, we plumb the depths of our soul in its greatest maturity. Nevertheless, despite Jesus's patient explanations, the kingdom of God remains a "riddle wrapped in a mystery inside an enigma." It's difficult enough for the enlightened to understand what Jesus is talking about. For those who do not choose to seek the kingdom, it can never be explained. Well-meaning humanists and the worldly wise simply have no idea what kingdom seekers are up to when they refuse to take revenge, or when they forgive their mortal enemies, or when they make their self-destructive calls for social justice. Kingdom seekers appear to be cracked in the head. "The wind blows where it chooses and you hear the sound of it, but you do not know where it comes from or where it goes. So it is with everyone who is born of the Spirit."

The Search for the Kingdom—the Ten Commandments

But where is this kingdom of God? It is certainly not found in the divine restaurants of New York City or on the sun-drenched beaches of Cannes. The kingdom is not found in a medieval nation-state, where the principles of religion are hard-wired into the secular law to enforce the coming of this very kingdom. The kingdom is not even found in the austere cloisters of the monastery, where devout people pray all their lives. God's kingdom is only found within the human soul loving other human souls. "Once Jesus was asked by the Pharisees when the kingdom of God was coming and he answered, "The kingdom of God is not coming with things that can be observed, nor will they say 'Look here it is!' or 'There it is!' For in fact the kingdom of God is among you" (Luke 17:20-21).

But how do we search for the kingdom of God? What are we supposed to do? The answer is found brilliantly condensed in all the riches of Jesus's prayer to the Father. And one way to understand this prayer is to compare it with the Ten Commandments, an ancient and integral part of Scripture. This may seem a surprising thing to do, but it can be very fruitful. After all, Jesus made it clear that he came to complete the Jewish law, not to render it obsolete. "Do not think that I have come to abolish the law or the prophets; I have come not to abolish but to fulfill. For truly I tell you, until heaven and earth pass away, not one letter, not one stroke of a letter will pass from the law until all is accomplished" (Matthew 5:17-18). That's why it's not really surprising to find that Jesus's prayer is built on the same structure as the Ten Commandments and holds much the same spiritual content, though the prayer and the Commandments are presented in radically different ways.

The Commandments are the dry bones of the kingdom—the white bleached skeleton of what is yet to be born. Jesus's prayer puts on the living flesh, which takes the shape of the skeleton but adds the beauty of a child or of a young woman or an ascetic hermit or a crone. An examination of the Commandments' skeleton and the prayer's flesh reveals not only their telling symmetry, but also the growth of God's spiritual policy over the thirteen hundred years of revelation that lie between them. What we see in all those fruitful centuries is the kingdom of God taking on its living beauty.

The Commandments were received by Moses on Mount Sinai. They form a basic code of moral laws written for a rough, nomadic people. They are minimalist and mostly negative. They require the listener to take his own action or else face the consequences. You! Do not commit adultery. You! Do not kill. You! Don't steal, ever. God does not come into this picture, except as the person who framed these compelling orders. In part, the Commandments are the simple rules against murder and theft that all Stone Age peoples tried to enforce, even in the most primitive of pagan societies. That's why it's apt that the Commandments were written on stone tablets. They come out of a Stone Age culture and, for instance, treat a woman as a man's property. "You shall not covet your neighbor's house; you shall not covet your neighbor's wife, or male or female slave, or ox, or donkey, or anything that belongs to your neighbor" (Exodus 20:1-17).

There is no equal prohibition against wives coveting other women's husbands. But the Ten Commandments move ahead of pagan law by proclaiming that the God of the Jews is unique and must be worshiped exclusively. They also include a peerless prohibition against spiritual crimes, such as lusting for things that belong to others, not only because these crimes of the heart may lead to actual crimes like theft or rape, but because they soil the person's spirit.

The parallels between the Ten Commandments and Jesus's prayer are intricately woven, like the tracery of bones in a skate. In fact, each of the Ten Commandments has its own twin petition in Jesus's prayer, and each Commandment and its twin—though they are written centuries apart—lies in the same position in each of the two compositions. The Commandments open with a declaration of powerful authority and powerful recognition of relationship: "I am the Lord your God who brought you out of the land of Egypt, out of the house of slavery. You shall have no other gods before me." That's the flat Mount Sinai forbiddance. And it's *sine qua non*. You cannot worship the one true God in any way at all without obeying the First Commandment given to Moses. In the same position in Jesus's prayer—at the very beginning—we find the corresponding act of spiritual awakening. We say "Father" and we recognize the uniqueness of the God portrayed in the First Commandment. But we also learn a lot more. *Father* tells us of God's abiding love for every single one of us, and for the nation of the world. The opening of Jesus's prayer embodies the First Commandment in full, and yet adds a hundred thousand miles of spirituality to it in our vigorous search for the coming of the kingdom of God.

The Second Commandment says "You shall not make wrongful use of the name of the Lord your God." Basically, this means "Don't use his name as a swear word, or to make false oaths." In the same position in Jesus's prayer, we find the other side of the coin: "Hallowed be thy name," which asks that people refrain from blaspheming. It also prays that all the world will come to know God's goodness and revere him. Instead of a thunderous twenty-five-word "don't dare do this" commandment that's understood in a flash, we have a gentle four-word petition that could take a whole lifetime of spirituality to explore as we search for the kingdom of God.

"Remember the Sabbath day and keep it holy," says the Third Commandment. In Jesus's prayer, we find "Thy kingdom come," which prays that God's kingdom will embrace everybody in his holiness and his love, not just on the Sabbath, but on every day of the week, forever.

The Commandments and the prayer arise out of the same divine provenance, but they come across in radically different ways. The Commandments are the absolute basic for a decent life. Once they are obeyed, the issue of lawlessness that originally gave rise to them is closed, for good. We live in obedience to God, and that's that. The petitions of Jesus's prayer also embody this law, but they build our spirituality continuously toward the coming of the kingdom, which does not arrive—yet. In all our lives, we never properly hallow God's name or trust him fully for our bread or truly forgive others. No matter how devoutly we say Jesus's prayer there is still a long way to travel toward the kingdom of God.

The Commandments and the prayer diverge in other ways. We obey the Commandments on our own initiative. We make no plea to God. We simply say "Okay. I will not kill" or "I will not steal." But in Jesus's prayer, we don't say "All right. I will hallow God's name." We say: "Please do this for us—Let your name be hallowed amongst us, through your own divine inspiration." In other words, "Come and help us Lord, to grow in your love." In the Commandments, we move forward under our own steam. In the prayer, we can only move forward with God's help as a partner and guide and the very source of our spirituality. That's a fundamental distinction. We can say the Commandments five hundred times, and the effect is always the same. But each time we say Jesus's prayer, the love of God grows powerfully within us and we take a new step toward the coming kingdom.

The Fourth Commandment says "Honor your father and your mother," and is again matched by "Father," the first petition of the prayer. "Father" honors our divine Father as a parent full of love, which reinforces our love for our own parents and strengthens our obedience to the Fourth Commandment. Many people who are alienated from their earthly father or mother may find it difficult, if not impossible, to recognize God as Father, but comparing the two is not really the point. Even the very best earthly mother or father is only a facsimile of the divine Father. That's why the prayer goes so much further than the Commandment.

The Fifth Commandment says "You shall not kill." It matches "Hallowed be thy name," which urges us not only to refrain from murder, but to treat all people as God the Father's sacred creation.

The Commandments and the prayer, taken together, reveal that God's plans for the coming of the kingdom are not just a rambling scriptural discourse through Exodus, Judges, Kings, and other blazing biblical books punctuated by a series of battles with idol worshippers, spectacular sins, howling prophets, and other entertaining or horrifying diversions. God's plan is consistent from beginning to end of Scripture—a sublime spiritual policy revealed step by step, from a time well before the Commandments to Jesus's teaching, his sacrifice, and his little prayer. With Jesus, the coming of the kingdom is finally put into place.

The correspondence between the Commandments and the prayer continues to the end of both. The last three Commandments mirror the last three petitions in Jesus's prayer. You've got to stop stealing (Seventh Commandment) before you can pray that all of us—me and my neighbors—will be given enough bread everyday and that we will all share it together. You can't steal bread for yourself and share your bread lovingly with a neighbor at the same time. That's a contradiction. And telling lies about our neighbors (Eighth Commandment) and coveting a man's wife and goods (Ninth and Tenth Commandments) are the acts of giving in to a destructive temptation. They match "And lead us not into temptation."

The search for the kingdom becomes even clearer when the tense of the verbs in the prayer and in the Commandments are compared. The Commandments are flat orders, expressed mostly in the negative imperative—thou shalt not do this, thou shalt not do that. Clearly "shall not" applies to choices in the future. When the temptation arises, the Commandments say, "Desist!" Jesus's prayer, on the other hand, makes a brilliant use of time to give us a greater understanding of what life is like in the presence of God, in the coming of the kingdom, right here and now.

The prayer reveals that the search for the kingdom of God is not tomorrow or next week or next year. It is always now. The first word, *Father,* is an explosive avowal of the eternal truth of God's love—now. We go on to ask for our "daily bread," that is to say our bread for now, not our bread for ten years from now. We ask for forgiveness and leadership ("Lead us not") right now, not tomorrow, so that we can cast off our anxieties in present time and reorient ourselves toward the search for the kingdom. The crowning petition, "Thy kingdom come," is also a prayer about the dynamic present. It makes us contemplate—today—the brilliance of God's kingdom, even though the kingdom is not here. This petition does not call for the establishment of the kingdom in 2008 or 8002 or in the end time. It calls for the "coming" of the kingdom, which is the mystical anticipation of the kingdom today, as well as its actual growth now in the human community, as we speak. The kingdom is not here yet, but the coming of the kingdom is categorically now, not later. What the prayer does so brilliantly is to root the person who is praying in the present, where God is, and where the person can be free of the burdens of the past and the future as he or she seeks the coming of the kingdom, today.

The prayer also roots us—not only in the now—but also in the here, the place where "I" stand right now. "Father" prompts us to open our eyes and look around, and we suddenly realize how very much God the Father has given us. We stop wanting a better house or a younger wife or a fancier car. We stop aching for the boisterous teenagers to leave home, and we no longer hanker for a new job with greater status or for more money. When we say "Father" we realize how much God has blessed us with wonderful gifts and fabulous people, all around us today. "Give us this day our daily bread" leads us into contentment with the simplest foods and the most basic comforts, which are usually found here, locally, and we stop hunting for exotic fruits and fashionable clothing brought from faraway places at great expense. "And lead us not into temptation" seeks to shield "me" from the temptation that lies all around me in this place, right now.

Jesus's prayer leads us firmly into the place where "I" am now, which becomes the center of the universe, and that is where God always resides—in the center. We are led firmly from where we had been going so disjointedly into the luminous here and the dynamic now. This is the living moment, the one we have been trying so hard to avoid with all our guilt about the past and our anxieties about what is yet to come. And when we find ourselves here in this place that we occupy and in this very moment in which we live, we start to appreciate the brilliant presence of God in this and every other second of our lives. In the here and now, the search for the kingdom finally becomes possible.

The Ten Commandments are the barbed wire fence that stops us from straying off the path into the minefield beyond that would blow us all up. Jesus's prayer is the open road lying beneath our feet, leading over the cloudless horizon toward the capital of the kingdom, a place of joy that we can barely imagine. What the prayer calls for is an appreciation of the spiritual brilliance of the here and now, a place where an infinite God plays hide-and-seek, shyly waiting to be found and crowned as King.

The Search for the Kingdom—Edmund G. Ross

The kingdom of God is close to all those people who do a good day's work for a fair wage. It is close to any man who loyally loves a woman, despite the blandishments of other comely women. The kingdom of God is close to those heroic nurses who care for people with colon cancer with love and grace. The kingdom of God is close to Colette, the British spy in France during World War II who refused to identify any of her colleagues, even after six months of torture at the hands of the Nazis. This woman died whole, despite all her misery and mutilation. The kingdom of God is close to all those who stand up for the truth or for decency or for peace, whether they are religious or not. Edmund G. Ross was one of these people.[7]

In 1868, President Andrew Johnson of the United States was under threat of impeachment. He had annoyed radicals in the Republican Party in Congress by seeking to rebuild the Southern states after the destruction of the American Civil War. The Republicans opposed him because they wanted to penalize the South for its attempt to secede from the Union and for the war that it had inflicted on the American people. But President Johnson didn't like this vengeful policy. He wanted the Civil War forgotten and the South rebuilt. President Johnson and Congress were also at loggerheads over other petty issues. Did the president really have the power to veto this bill or that bill? The radicals demanded to know. Did Johnson overreach his office when he dismissed the secretary of war from his cabinet because the secretary sympathized with the radicals? And so on, until the relationship between the president and Congress broke down.

The radicals set out to impeach Johnson. To succeed, they needed two-thirds of the votes in the Senate. And they were confident of getting almost the right number. The only question mark was Edmund G. Ross, a new senator from Kansas. But Ross had a promising history, in their eyes. He had opposed slavery and even freed some slaves, so he was thought to be opposed to reconciliation with the slave-happy South. But nobody knew for sure, because Ross wasn't talking. In *Profiles of Courage,* John F. Kennedy wrote:

> Ross and his fellow doubtful Republicans were daily pestered, spied upon and subjected to every form of pressure [to vote for impeachment.] Their residences were carefully watched, their social circles suspiciously scrutinized, and their every move and [all their] companions secretly marked in special notebooks. They were warned in the party press, harangued by their

constituents, and sent dire warnings threatening political ostracism and even assassination [if they did not toe the line].[8]

When the impeachment proceedings began, the gallery of Congress was packed with excited people, who had come to see this historic event. By this time, with the hour of resolution at hand, the radicals only needed Ross's vote to secure a majority and impeach Johnson. Each senator in the chamber was asked to vote aloud, one by one. Ross said later that when it came to his turn: "I almost literally looked down into my open grave. Friendships, position, fortune, everything that makes life desirable to an ambitious man were about to be swept away by the breath of my mouth, perhaps forever."[9] Ross voted "Not guilty" and blocked Johnson's impeachment. One historian said it was "the most heroic act in American history, incomparably more difficult than any deed of valor upon the field of battle."[10] Others echoed Cicero, who said centuries earlier that "There are... instances of civic courage that are not inferior to the courage of the soldier. Indeed, [they] call for even greater energy and even greater devotion."[11]

Ross later explained his decision. First of all, he did not think the president was guilty as charged. So impeachment would not have been just. And if Johnson had been made to step down, the office of president would have been irreparably harmed. "This government had never faced so insidious a danger,"[12] Ross concluded. The precious balance of power between Congress and president would have been destroyed, and power shifted heavily toward Congress. In the end, Ross's courageous and principled stand ruined his political career forever.

The search for the kingdom of God is not only conducted in church or on one's knees at prayer. It is conducted everywhere, at all times.

One Woman's Search for the Kingdom

In the mid-1980s, a woman named Gloria Daysi Alonzo Jaimes spent much of her time working with the unemployed in El Salvador. She helped impoverished women by training them in skills they might be able to use to gain work and feed their families. Jaimes knew her work would be viewed as treason by the ruling right-wing elite. Social activists were always viewed balefully in El Salvador, even if they were not politically minded. These bleeding-heart liberals had to be organizing resistance against the government, the authorities told themselves, otherwise why were they mingling with the wretched? Simple kindness is never countenanced by paranoid right-wing governments clinging to power against the wishes of the people. Helping the unemployed was subversion in El Salvador and was not to be tolerated. Jaimes knew all this and continued her work.

According to a report[13] in the *Globe and Mail*, a Canadian newspaper, Jaimes was captured by the terror squads and imprisoned. She was beaten on the head, stomach, and back while blindfolded so that she could not anticipate the blows, and while handcuffed tightly so that she could not resist. This torture went on for days, she told Karen Rudd, a Canadian social worker. Then the punishment was escalated. Jaimes was raped repeatedly by the prison guards and then treated to the singular pleasure of the capucha, a form of torture common in El Salvador at the time. A rubber hood filled with caustic lime powder was placed over her head and tied around her neck so that no air could be drawn in. Then she was beaten hard to force her to gasp for air. But the capucha contained only lime, which burned her lungs and throat and left permanent damage. When Jaimes passed out, coughing in great pain and suffocating, she was resuscitated by electric shock or a bucket of water, and the torture was started all over again. In all, she was given the capucha six times, until she was utterly drained and terrified. This treatment was intended as a nasty warning to Jaimes to stay out of politics, or at least the practice of politics as it was viewed by the ruling elite at that time.

After a month, Jaimes was released by her captors, who were confident that they had tortured some common sense into her. She returned to her work with the unemployed, now knowing only too well the risks. Soon she was picked up again, gang-raped by the death squads, tortured to death, and dumped as garbage on the edge of the city. But Jaimes had taken Jesus's words to heart—the search for the kingdom of God is more important than any other consideration, even the loss of an eye, a right arm, good health, or life itself.

The Search for the Kingdom of God—the Afghans[14]

The search for the kingdom of God reached one of its peaks in Afghanistan in the mid-1980s. From December 27, 1979, onward, the army of the Soviet

Union tried to bring Afghanistan under military control in order to support a puppet regime in the capital, Kabul. But many Afghans would not accept Communist rule because they were Muslim and abhorred the Russians' "dialectical materialism." Rule by atheists would be a blasphemy, a stain on the honor of God among his people. The Afghans felt they must preserve God's kingdom amongst them.

The farmers and shepherds of the Afghan hills declared themselves holy warriors and fought the Russians with whatever weapons they could obtain—a few Stinger missiles from the United States, who didn't want to be directly involved, a few machine guns stolen from Russian bases, and a motley collection of rifles proudly handmade by village blacksmiths.

The center of the struggle was the great, sweeping Panjshir Valley in the north, a swath of arid plain lying between mountains, one that commanded the main supply routes between the USSR and Kabul. The Russians tried to intimidate the Afghans with a reign of terror. They assaulted the valley's inhabitants with poison gas, chemicals, and the most diabolical means of all, booby traps that looked like toys, which attracted and maimed the warriors' children. From time to time, Russian soldiers entered a village on the valley floor and slit the throats of the children's mothers, leaving them to bleed to death in the snow. Their aim was to demoralize the fierce warriors in the hills—the loving fathers and husbands of the victims in the valley.

Friendless and poorly armed, the Afghan shepherds seemed to have little hope of success against the might of the Soviet Union. But when they fought the Russians and their puppet government, they did not publicly beg for victory or plead for the divine assistance they so desperately needed. They asserted the majesty of the Godhead with an ancient Islamic cry: "God is Great! God is Merciful!" This is not a prayer for divine mercy. It is the declaration of a fact that will still be true even if the Afghans are beaten. "God is Great! God is Merciful!" The Afghans would either live in God's kingdom on Earth, or die in it. Nothing else was acceptable.

The Russians and the Afghans present a striking contrast. The atheistic Communists were insecure within the boundaries of the biggest country on Earth, with awesome military power under their control. But they had to control Afghanistan in order to feel safe on their southern border. The Afghans were so secure in their trust in God they were able to place at risk everything they owned to defend his good name. Their praise of the

Godhead, and his apparently nonexistent mercy, seems ironic, even comical. But the Afghans believed they were declaring a spiritual truth that transcends any misfortune they would ever experience. Their security lay not in power, nor in any promises requested or received, nor even in life itself, but in the greatness of the God they served. "God is Great! God is Merciful!"

Jesus taught the same lesson. Real security lies only in the search for the kingdom of God.

> "Therefore, I tell you, do not worry about your life, what you will eat or what you will drink, or about your body, what you will wear. Is not life more than food, and the body more than clothing? Look at the birds of the air; they neither sow nor reap, nor gather into barns, and yet your heavenly Father feeds them. Are you not of more value than they? And can any of you by worrying add a single hour to your span of life?... Therefore do not worry saying 'What will we eat?' or 'What will we drink?' or 'What will we wear?' For it is the Gentiles who strive for all these things; and indeed your heavenly Father knows that you need all these things. But strive first for the kingdom of God and his righteousness, and all these things will be given to you as well." Matthew 6:25-27, 31-33

The Afghans were faced with this same choice—the conspicuous security of material things, or the real, hidden safety of the kingdom of God. And the Russian blandishments were tempting. Afghan villages that submitted to Soviet rule received the comforts of food and medication, clean water, and modern education. The Russians presented a compassionate face to compliant Afghans, because they would have liked to convince the world of Communism's fatherly concern for the masses. If they could have properly subdued Afghanistan, the Russians would undoubtedly have modernized the entire countryside. They would have brought it out of the religious Middle Ages into the twentieth century—and atheism.

The Afghans faced a hard choice: food laced with the poison of atheism, or the glory of the kingdom of God, which in that place meant pain, suffering, and death. But the Afghans understood an important truth: securing food and medicine serves only an illusory physical reality. What the Afghans sought was greater—service to God and reliance upon him for all their well-being and all their fate. The search for the kingdom is more concrete than bread and insulin, they believed, because it engages the whole person, body and soul, mind and spirit.

Jesus promised food and clothing to those who seek the kingdom, but also other, less-understood benefits. "Blessed are the poor in spirit, for theirs is the kingdom of heaven. Blessed are those who mourn, for they will be comforted. Blessed are the meek, for they will inherit the earth" (Matthew 5:3-5). But wait. Can this last declaration really be true? Jesus's promise to the meek seems to fly in the face of history and human experience. Most of the earth is "inherited" by great empires and by arrogant, wealthy people. The humble seem to harvest only poverty and humiliation.

Jesus's strange promise can be tested hard in places like the Panjshir Valley.

The question of God's kingdom and the inheritance of the earth can be sharpened. Who inherited the valley through the spirit, directly from the hands of the God that made it and continues to refresh its beauty every moment? The answer must be the warrior shepherds, because only they can enjoy the valley in all its majesty—material, mystical, and spiritual. The mountain tribesmen are the valley's heirs precisely because they have given up possession of it, which they might have enjoyed in partnership with those who have repudiated the valley's creator. The holy warriors cling to the valley with nothing but faith. And they are rewarded with the only real ownership.

Jesus's promise becomes clearer. The earth is more than soil and mountains, trees and rivers. It is a looking glass that reflects the magnificence of its creator, if the person looking has a true spiritual disposition. The earth is an inheritance that is always there to solace and comfort those who are not proud. It is an inheritance that is never taken, only given, and then only as a fleeting impression of the infinite beauty of the Creator. What the humble receive is a brilliant vision of God in his kingdom, which is exactly what they seek. It is a gift that cannot be taken away by all the armies and all the weapons in the world.

The Afghans may have inherited the earth in a mystical sense, but did Jesus's promise to kingdom seekers also have a practical meaning? The Russians were defeated in 1988 and withdrew, licking the many wounds inflicted on this mighty nation by these devout and primitive people. Today, Afghanistan continues to be plagued by brutal contests between the godly and the ungodly. The kingdom comes. The kingdom goes. The kingdom retreats and the kingdom comes. It is the same all over the world, all the time.

The Search for the Kingdom

The search for the kingdom of God is the greatest of all adventures and the farthest of journeys. It travels light-years beyond science, which can figure out the way the universe works and powerfully manipulate it, but gives no final insight into its origins or what it really stands for. The search for the kingdom travels beyond metaphysics, which can look behind nature cleverly and entertain the intellect, but in the end is impotent. A person cannot reach out to God while arguing about whether God really exists. The search for the kingdom of God lies beyond theology, which explores the actions of the Godhead respectfully, but engages only the mind and not the heart. The search for the kingdom is the mind and the heart and the whole person in motion, traveling to the origin of all things—the Godhead.

The divine King is not found in the vastness of the galaxy or in the intricacy of the atom, which are finite, nor even in the tangle of our ever-active minds. The King lives beyond this world in the fastnesses of infinity. He can only be reached out there in the forever land, through other people of the human community, which either does or does not become the divine kingdom, depending on whether the individual and the group embrace the distant and immanent King.

The search for the kingdom is more than studious contemplation or reading and interpreting the Bible. It is a plan of bold, relentless action in favor of a person and the people. Jesus's simple petition, prayed and practiced often, "Thy kingdom come," takes the adventurer closer and closer to the eternal city, which grows ever more sublime and mysterious as it draws nearer. This prayer is a journey whose destination has been well reported, but one that is barely imagined.

5

The Other Side

After passing over the pinnacle of "Thy kingdom come," Jesus's prayer changes sharply in character, in the way that a mountain may have two different appearances on the north and the south slopes. On the north face, the first three petitions constitute a search for the coming of the kingdom. We acknowledge God as Father, ascend toward heaven by hallowing God's name, and finally seek the coming of the kingdom that is the high destiny of all human beings. This part of the prayer reveals what the individual and the community owe to God by way of recognition, but have not been paying to him down in the low mire of sinfulness. It asks that this account be paid in full, with God's help, as the kingdom comes.

On the other side of "Thy kingdom come," we place all our faith in the God we now know to provide us with what we need on the rest of our journey. Bread represents all the necessities of life. Forgiveness is requested after bread because forgiveness is academic for the starving. Finally, we seek leadership as we go on our way. Spiritual guidance is sought last because we can't focus on the way ahead until we lose the distractions of hunger and guilt.

What we ask for on this side of the prayer is also the three basics provided by any good business manager. First, the employee is given the energy to do the job (bread). Then he is given a sense of personal worth (through forgiveness of his faults), and finally, energized in full, he is given inspired leadership in the direction of the company's goals. But this is a petition to God, not to a company president. And these three requests also rise in spiritual dignity. First, we ask for coarse material things, then we ask for the spiritual liberation of forgiveness, and finally we beg for the total security of leadership by God himself. By the end of the prayer we have everything we could possibly need—from the most earthly to the most spiritual—all received in the right order.

But the lesson of human fellowship remains constant. The person praying is always heroically identified with the community. He prays for food for everybody, not just himself: "Give *us* bread." He prays that God, and all individual men and women, will pour out forgiveness to one another: "Forgive us... as we forgive others." And he prays that he and all people everywhere will follow God's leadership and conquer temptation: "lead us not." In the first half of the prayer, we go to God, with his help. In the second half, God bends down to all of us, graciously, in answer to our requests.

The prayer's second phase can be viewed in another light. In the first half, we identify the three persons of the Trinity—Father, High Priest, and King. In the second half, we ask each of these three persons to provide us with what is consistent with their special relationship with us—the Father provides birth and nurture (bread); the High Priest dispenses forgiveness; and the King delivers leadership. But we do not say the prayer as a series of couplets: "Father, Give us bread" followed by "Thy kingdom come" and "lead us not into temptation." That would seem to be insincere. "Okay, I'll call you Father, and then maybe I'll get what I really want, some bread, etc."

The grace of this prayer is that it first turns our full attention to God in all three persons until our homage of the divine is complete. Once we have arrived in God's embrace, we ask him for what we need, and what we receive flows from God, as grace from him, not as a grasping request from us. Also, our sense of spiritual proportion is preserved because we ask for our needs only after we have broken our obsession with our self by focusing on God. In the light of this new understanding of God's love, gained in the first part of the prayer, we have a much better sense of what we really need and should ask for in the second half.

In going to God and placing faith in him for all one's needs, the person praying is close to becoming what Jesus calls "poor in spirit." And in the

Sermon on the Mount, Jesus made this solemn promise: "Blessed are the poor in spirit for theirs is the kingdom of heaven." In the second half of the prayer, the poor do not stand in the kingdom of God, because that is yet to come, but for the moment we stand within the coming of the kingdom, because that can be here and now.

6

Give Us This Day Our Daily Bread

God will provide whatever bread we need, the Scriptures tell us. And that is one reason Jesus calls the first person of the Godhead Father. He begot us out of nothing and cares for us with bread and other provisions. But there are a multitude of mysteries behind this fatherliness of God. If we are to probe this iron promise of sustenance, we must ask how God provides bread, and when.

Will bread be provided by miracle, when we pray? Apparently, nothing can be ruled out. "For truly I tell you, if you have faith the size of a mustard seed, you will say to this mountain, 'Move from here to there' and it will move; and nothing will be impossible for you" (Matthew 17:20). Calling up bread by means of faith would seem to be child's play compared to moving millions of tons of rock. But few people hold a granite of faith that can withstand the earthquake of fear or skepticism. But even if our faith lacks stuffing, God the Father will not brush it aside. That's why Jesus advises us to say "Father... Give us this day our daily bread."

But how does this divine care actually work? And how does it fit in with the laws of nature we think we understand so well in the twenty-first century? Does God the Father make bread appear out of nothing when nobody is watching? Does he answer our prayers through unseen miracles that break apart the inner workings of matter? These seem to be unnecessarily exotic propositions. Instead, does God the Father work through the laws of nature? Is he at the heart of the material world, orchestrating it for his own ends and for ours, invisible to us all? This question is not as unanswerable as it may seem.

Father, Give Us Bread!

God the Father does care for us, most of the time, through the laws of science rather than through miracles. And Jesus's prayer confirms this conclusion. "Father" tells us that God existed before humankind, because a father always predates his children. "Father" also declares that God must have built the "family home" in which we live—the environment of the natural world. Therefore, he must have designed the laws of nature. "Father" coupled with "Give us this day our daily bread" tells us more. It insists that God works every day through this natural world to feed us and nourish us. If this were not true, "Give us bread" would be a pointless prayer, a mockery instigated by Jesus against the hungry. And if we believe that, Christianity is a charade.

"Father" and "Give us bread" tell us that the ultimate power in the universe is not mechanical or scientific or random. It is personal, even political, and always political in our favor, the way a parent is. In some mysterious way, Einstein's famous equation $e = mc^2$ is not a cold, detached truth. It is a personal decision of some kind, a carefully chosen tool of the Father to reach his mysterious ends, which include providing his children with bread. The same conclusion can be reached through science, though incompletely, because science is only a study of the automobile's motor. It gives us no information about the driver or his destination. But science still suggests there is a driver in the car.

The universe that science knows so well contains a billion trillion stars with their myriad of moons and orbiting rocks. The stars are million-degree furnaces, but they are still only pinpoints in the universe, barely filling four-hundredths of its space. This star-twinkled universe cavern is huge and ancient. It is more than 7 billion light-years across and 18 billion years old. Where does it come from? Scientists offer one explanation that says eons ago, a massively dense protosubstance exploded in a big bang, which made it swell into the ever-expanding universe. But where did this royal jelly come from? And what triggered the big bang that started the clock of time? Science is coming tantalizingly close to an answer that is almost biblical.

All matter is made up of almost the same amounts of positive and negative charges, according to K. C. Cole in her book, *The Hole in the Universe*. If all these charged particles in the universe of opposite polarity were to collide, they would annihilate each other into almost nothing, she says.[1] This intelligence suggests the universe started as a cataclysmic division of nothing into two opposite charges, with a few wrinkles thrown in that we don't yet understand. This vision of time's first moment finds an echo in the scientifically ignorant book of Genesis: "In the beginning, when God created the heavens and the earth, the earth was a formless void and darkness covered the face of the deep... and God separated the light from the darkness" (Genesis 1:1-4). If the ancient author were alive today, he might say: "In the beginning, God divided nothing into positive and negative to create all the heavens and the earth."

The idea that nothing was cut into two halves begs for a belief in an all-powerful being standing outside the universe with a razor-sharp cleaver. Science and theology appear to converge, and that embittered Robert Jastrow, an agnostic astronomer, in 1978. "For the scientist who has lived by his faith in the power of reason, the story [of recent discoveries] ends like a bad dream. He has scaled the mountains of ignorance, he is about to conquer the highest peak; as he pulls himself over the final rock, he is greeted by a band of theologians, who have been sitting there for centuries."[2]

The hand of God is not only visible in the universe's birth. It is discernible everywhere today. "Everything in the universe moves through the four-dimensional fabric of space and time at exactly the same speed—the speed of light," says Cole. "No matter what is moving, or how fast, change in motion through space-time remains absolutely zero—no matter what."[3] If space and time are locked together in this way, they cannot be nothing, in and of themselves. Space is not just the gap between objects, nor time just change. The space-time continuum must be a concrete reality, divided into its two components by our perception. But what is space-time, and where does it come from? This is one of three key mysteries that go beyond the reach of science.

The second mystery is the universe's dynamism, which is called energy and fires volcanoes, melts snow, and drives thousands of stones around Saturn, giving the appearance of rings from far away. Energy is also fashioned by powerful forces into the particles of what we call matter, the way a chef rolls suet pastry into little dumplings and puts them in a stew. In this way, energy makes up all the atoms of cats, catapults, and caterpillars. But where does it come from? Science cannot tell us.

The third mystery is the universe's iron policies, such as the law of gravity, the rules of thermodynamics, and the dance code of the weak force within the atom. These unbreakable rules subject all energy, everywhere, to servitude. A curve ball goes in a curve because of these rules. Good eyesight depends on these rules; so does loss of sight. How did these rules, or laws, or necessities, or whatever you call them, come to be? Why do they operate the way they do? Once again, science has no answer.

These three great fundamentals—energy, space-time, and policy—constitute the boundary wall of the universe, over which science cannot look. At this boundary we are left with many mysteries. Who or what holds space-time, energy, and law in their places, moment by moment? Who or what inserts new space into the universe as it gets bigger and as its galaxies become separated by greater distances? Space is not nothing, and there is no evidence that as the universe expands, space stretches. It's the same with time. Who or what provides time as the universe continues into the future? Time is not nothing, so new time must come from somewhere.

And what is the universe for? At large, it is flagrantly hostile to human life. Suns are so hot they would melt approaching spaceships. Many planets are airless, barren of vegetation, and immensely cold. Distances are so vast they distort time itself, until only the greatest human intellects can understand what goes on. At the other end of the scale, the very small is complex beyond our intellects, and stupefying in its bafflement. Atoms of iron and tin and carbon, so commonly found on earth, are so intricate that scientists cannot write equations to describe them. Each new particle of these atoms, as it is discovered, seems to be the final floor of matter for a few years, until it is split into smaller particles, apparently ad infinitum. Molecules are made up of atoms. Atoms are made up of protons. Protons are made up of quarks. Will this downward journey ever end? The microuniverse is not subhuman. It is superhuman.

In both the vast reaches of the universe and in the very small, reality goes about its business, beyond the grasp of the human mind and the span of the human body. But as the universe comes closer to human scale, it becomes benign. The billion hydrogen bombs exploding in the sun quietly warm the surface of the earth and make it livable. Travel on earth involves no detectable distortion of time as we plod around on horses and bicycles. A potato plant is a complex biological machine relying on elaborate microchemistry, but it is easy for a peasant to grow spuds. When the very small bunches up into the human world, it comes down to our dimensions. And when the very large is cut into small pieces, it bows down to human grasp. The place that humans occupy is an island of solicitude. Here, where we live, the world mutes its magnificence and panders to human life, sheltering us from the Creator's colossal energy and intimidating intellect.

Jesus's prayer tells us that the origin of all the universe's components, big and small, is God the Father, the One who built the family home, with its cozy living room and its uninhabitable attic and basement. Jesus's prayer does not claim humankind is the center of the universe, or that the universe was made primarily with us in mind. But "Father" does say that whatever mysterious plans God has for the world, they include our wellbeing. In the mysteries of the universe, we can vaguely make out the luminous shadow of God the Father, and we can see the glimmerings of a good reason to confidently say "Father... Give us this day our daily bread." But we can't trace the movement of bread from the hands of God into our mouths. That is not part of the deal.

Bread in Malta in 1940–1942

"Bread! Father! Give us a little bread," was the urgent prayer of the Maltese people during World War II as they slipped into famine.[4] The second Great Siege of Malta began when the Italian air force started bombing the island on June 11, 1940. Benito Mussolini's airmen were soon joined by the German Luftwaffe based in nearby Sicily. Within two years, this tiny Mediterranean island became the most bombed place on Earth and endured the longest siege in the history of the world. Yet, against all odds, Malta survived. The outcome turned on the faith of the Maltese and their persistent prayers to God the Father, as well as the courage of the military defenders, which is maybe what God the Father inspired in them in response to the prayers of the Maltese.

> And he said to them, "Suppose one of you has a friend, and you go to him at midnight and say to him, 'Friend lend me three loaves of bread; for a friend of mine has arrived, and I have nothing to set before him.' And he answers, from within, 'Do not bother me, the door has already been locked, and my children are with me in bed; I cannot get up and give you anything.'

I tell you even though he will not get up and give him anything because he is his friend, at least because of his persistence he will get up and give him whatever he needs. So I say to you: Ask, and it will be given you; search, and you shall find; knock, and the door will be opened for you." Luke 11:5-9

Besieged Malta was a British colony in an Italian sea during World War II. The main island is only nineteen miles long, and the whole population of Malta is only 400,000 people, almost all of whom are Catholics. When the bombs started falling, the Maltese were terrified. They fled the coastal cities into the center of the island and sheltered in farmhouses, packed ten to a room. The churches were full all day long. Processions of the Blessed Sacrament wound their way through the narrow streets and were met by throngs of people saying the rosary aloud on their knees. At that time, the Royal Air Force maintained only a few obsolete Gloster Gladiator aircraft on the island. These out-of-date fighters rose valiantly against the Italian bombers but left few scars. Soon, there were only three left. The ever-devout Maltese named them *Faith, Hope,* and *Charity.*

The German and Italian air forces attacked Malta because it straddled the sea lanes from Italy to North Africa, the routes over which ships loaded with soldiers and armaments supplied Field Marshal Erwin Rommel as his armies gained ground against the British army in the desert war. The Axis powers feared the island would be used as a base from which British aircraft could bomb their ships. That's why Malta had to be crushed. In Sicily, only sixty miles away—a short bombing run—the Italian air force was soon joined by the German Luftwaffe and together they tried to bomb Malta into either submission or oblivion. But they reckoned without the faith of the Maltese, the dedication of the British fliers, and apparently, the supreme will of God the Father.

By June 11, 1942, Malta had experienced 2,537 air raids—far more than any city in heavily bombed Britain. The longest raid lasted continuously for five months, with bombs dropping on the island hour after hour, day and night, heaping devastation upon the destruction. The bombs ravaged Valletta, the capital, and most other cities as well. But as the bombardment intensified, the mood of the people changed. On weekends the shores were crowded with bathers, and when the sirens went off, anyone seen sneaking away to a shelter was booed. And every morning the Maltese dock workers valiantly turned up for work in the ruined harbor. The Maltese had already proven during the first Great Siege of Malta by the Turks in 1565 that they could accept almost unendurable hardship in defense of their rocky, semibarren island. The Commonwealth pilots—half starved because of the siege—demonstrated superhuman determination in preventing the Axis powers from gaining total control of the air.

By August 1942, Malta was only four weeks away from defeat. When supplies of food were exhausted, the choice would be famine or surrender. The situation seemed hopeless. In four months, seventeen relief ships had set out from both ends of the Mediterranean for Malta and only two had arrived. When the food ran out, the tiny garrison of British soldiers led by Lord Gort resolved to invade Sicily by themselves and die fighting in order to declare, finally, the gallantry of Malta's defiance.

Meanwhile, the unarmed Maltese relied on their prayers. The churches were full, but not silent, as the excitable Maltese loudly delivered their supplications to God and all the saints with passion. And if anything, as the situation became more desperate, their faith became more brazen. They appealed to the Father directly through Matthew's prayer, "Missierna, li inti fis-smewwiet.... Hobzna ta' kuljum aghtina llum" [Our Father who art in heaven.... Give us this day our daily bread]. And they prayed to the Father through the mother of the Son. "O Maiden Lady of Victory, Queen of Heaven and Earth, gather the bombs into your mantle, and deliver us from the attack."[5] The bombs continued to fall, but the prayers were not wasted.

Britain decided to make one last, desperate effort to break the siege. A huge convoy was formed in Gibraltar at the western end of what was now "the Italian sea." The convoy consisted of fourteen merchant ships loaded with food and supplies. They were escorted by two Royal Navy battleships, three aircraft carriers, seven cruisers, and thirty-two destroyers. The size of the flotilla was an attempt at its protection, but it meant the convoy was too big to sneak through by stealth. It would become a sitting duck. In *The Hinge of Fate,* Winston Churchill wrote: "It should have been within the enemy's power...to destroy this convoy utterly."[6] But a quarrel arose between the Germans and the Italians on how to deal with the convoy, which reduced their effectiveness.

The vessels came on for days through minefields, burning sister ships, and relentless attacks by aircraft, submarines, and fast surface raiders. All the vessels suffered, but the enemy paid special attention to the oil tanker USS *Ohio*, which was on loan from the American company Texaco and was loaded to capacity with aviation fuel for the Spitfires now on the island. *Ohio* was soon hit by a torpedo, which knocked out its steering gear and made it a straggler, even more vulnerable to attack. It was then bombed repeatedly, crash-dived by enemy aircraft that had been shot down, and, with its explosive cargo, forced to sail through blazing fuel oil spilled by other ships in their death throes.

Ohio became fit only for towing, and then not even manageable under tow. The crew abandoned ship. But Captain D. W. Mason had argued in a comfortable armchair in a London club that it was possible to get a ship through to Malta despite the Italians and Germans. That's probably why the British Admiralty assigned him to the task. After abandoning what seemed to be a doomed vessel, Captain Mason returned with volunteers. *Ohio* was then strapped between two Royal Navy destroyers to act as splints for her wayward hull. A third destroyer was attached astern to act as a rudder. In this way, *Ohio* limped, mortally wounded, into Grand Harbor.

The author Nicholas Monsarrat reconstructed the scene in *The Kappillan* [Parish Priest] *of Malta:*

> After the cheering there came a hush, as the people on watch gradually took in the details of what they had been staring at. It was the wreck of a very large tanker... [which] seemed to be sinking foot by foot as she approached the quay.... The watchers on the bastions had seen the four other [crippled ships] in the convoy come in... but this last survivor had taken more terrible punishment than all the others put together. She had her own cavernous torpedo-hole, under a mass of twisted plating at the bows, and another further aft. Her decks were ploughed up from end to end, as if the world's biggest can-opener had been at work, and some of her derricks were canted like saplings after a storm. On the fire-charred upper deck, amid a tangle of piping, two separate scrap heaps of metal, which were crashed aircraft still smoldering, added a freak element to the disaster. The tanker was so low in the water, so mortally wounded that a man could be seen sitting on deck and trailing his fingers in Grand Harbor.[7]

But *Ohio* was towed to Parlatorio Wharf to rest on an undersea wreck while she was unloaded, and none of her cargo of aviation fuel was lost.

This seemingly doomed convoy brought the Maltese a little food that came on the other ships, but also what they might never have admitted they wanted most—the fuel to continue their air war against the enemy's Mediterranean supply lines. Forever after, this "miraculous" deliverance has been celebrated among the Maltese as the Santa Marija Convoy, because it arrived on August 15, the feast of the Assumption of the Blessed Virgin

Mary into heaven as queen of angels and saints—the very person to whom they had directed many of their passionate prayers. And the Santa Marija Convoy was the turning point in the island's relief, perhaps even in the war itself, after Rommel lost the desert war, hampered by Malta's harassment of his supplies. To honor the devotion of the Maltese, King George VI awarded the George Cross, the highest civilian medal for bravery, to the entire population of Malta and later visited the island in person.

Jesus tells us that the Father grants all true prayers, though not necessarily quickly. The petitioner may have to repeat his or her prayer persistently like the Maltese. "Father, Give us this day our daily bread. Father, Give us... bread." "I am not a very religious man," says Milo Vassallo, Consul-General of Malta in Canada, a man who lived through the siege as a child. "But I firmly believe we were not conquered because of our prayers. The odds were so much against us."

Bread Miracles in Scripture

The delivery of bread to Malta was not a miracle in the normal sense of the word. But Scripture tells us that God did perform many bread miracles in answer to the faith of his needy followers. Manna fell from heaven for the Israelites and loaves were multiplied for both Elisha and Jesus. If we are to appreciate Scripture's lessons in full, we must embrace these miracles as one of a piece with the simple lessons about the kingdom of God that we call the parables.

The miracles that provide people with bread, good health, and other fine things add to the parables a romantic element that engages our childlike sense of wonder. Jesus, the bold knight, conquers the evil dragon of leprosy for a wretched woman. Jesus the good magician drives devils out of a man and sends them into a herd of pigs where they always belonged. Jesus, the sage, tells his devoted followers where to cast their nets in the sea to find fish. Jesus walks on water, as an invitation to an utterly illogical but completely trusting faith.

These are stories finer than *Harry Potter* or *The Chronicles of Narnia*, which may, in fact, derive their origin as literary forms from the history of miracles. The difference is that *Harry Potter* is fiction, but the Scripture's miracles are true. How are they true? In this age of science, can they be said to be actual historical facts? The answer is no, because facts are chunks of material reality and represent the action of natural law. "The sky is blue" is a fact. "John kissed Mary" is another. But God is not a fact. God is a reality that transcends the world, and his existence is a truth, not a fact. Miracles contravene the laws of science, so they cannot be called facts, either. Does this mean they are pure invention? No. Miracles are best described as true insights into historical facts that are now unknown. The miracles represent a mystery, one into which we cannot go any further. But the miracles are still true. At the same time, they are magical stories for the child within us. Yet they also nourish us as adults. The miracles in the Bible teach us profound lessons that are part and parcel of the deeper truths of Christianity and cannot be cut out of the whole without tearing the fabric of wisdom.

So what is the meaning of the miracles performed by Jesus and the prophets? Are they weighty one-off spectacles that took place in the year 700 B.C. or A.D. 30, to be reported devoutly, nodded at sagely, and forgotten? Or are they a series of flags stuck in the desert floor of our humanity to mark the underground watercourse of God's quietly flowing solicitude for all of us, as it continues mysteriously down the ages? Perhaps each miracle can be likened to a fireworks display organized to mark the two thousandth anniversary of an ancient nation-state. This one-day pyrotechnic treat reminds all the citizens not only that it's party time today, but also that they have a happy future in what otherwise seems to be a troubled country. In this way, the miracles reassure us.

A miracle can be likened to a mountain peak looming through the fog, or to the startling discovery of the egg-laying mammals of Australia, which warn us not to be too complacent about our knowledge of how nature allegedly works and who works it. Miracles are pointers to something extraordinary that goes on behind the ordinary screen of the natural world. That's why they are called supernatural. And there are miracles still today, miracles of mysterious healing and divine solicitude and the strange aid of saints. The age of miracles is not over yet. But in this age of science and skepticism, we don't talk about miracles any more.

Why Miracles?

The great legends in the first part of the Bible, such as the flood that covered the whole earth, come to an end, perhaps, with the parting of the waters of the sea of reeds to allow the Israelites to escape the Egyptian army. Or perhaps they end at the parting of the Jordan to allow the Israelites into the promised land. Wherever they end, the legends give way to accounts of the lives of ordinary people, punctuated with miracles. The miracles begin, perhaps, with the provision of manna to the Israelites wandering in the desert.

> Then the Lord said to Moses, "I am going to rain bread from heaven for you, and each day the people shall go out and gather enough for that day. In that way I will test them, whether they will follow my instruction or not. On the sixth day, when they prepare what they bring in, it will be twice as much as they gather on other days." Exodus 16:4-5

Friday's take was twice Saturday's because the Israelites were not allowed to work on the Sabbath, and God would never force them to do that, the good book says.

Was this provision of bread a miracle, and if so, what laws of science did it transcend? Many biologists speculate that manna was an edible fungus growing in the desert. The maverick Russian scientist Immanuel Velikovsky argued that the "fine flaky substance" was edible carbohydrates that condensed from the tail of a comet passing close to earth. This manna rained down onto the desert just when the Israelites happened to be hungry.[8] So was this a miracle? Are we even asking the right question? Is it a miracle if a natural event occurs fortuitously? Or is it only a happy coincidence? Whatever the science, the Scripture tells us that God the Father provided bread for the people of Israel by means that were either miraculous or mundane.

God is not parsimonious with his favors, either. Bread means more to God than just a ration of baked dough. "The rabble among them had a strong craving; and the Israelites also wept again and said, 'If only we had meat to eat. We remember the fish we used to eat in Egypt for nothing, the cucumbers, the melons, the leeks, the onions, and the garlic, but now our strength is dried up, and there is nothing at all but this manna to look at'"(Numbers 11:4-6). In a certain Texas prison, one punishment for breaking the rules is baked beans every meal for a month. This dire diet usually has the desired disciplinary effect. The Bible makes it clear that God does not want to inflict this kind of brutal breakfast boredom on anybody. "Then a wind went out from the Lord, and it brought quails from the sea and let them fall beside the camp, about a day's journey on this side and a day's journey on the other side, all around the camp, about two cubits [one yard] deep on the ground" (Numbers 11:31). "Give us this day our daily bread" is also apparently a prayer for a balanced diet.

More Bread Miracles

Much later, in the era of the Jewish kings, the prophet Elijah saved the life of the starving widow of Zarephath and her son by faith alone. The widow had a jar with a little meal in it and a jar with some oil, and nothing else. She was preparing to die. But Elijah told her: "For thus says the Lord the God of Israel: the jar of meal will not be emptied and the jug of oil will not fail until the day that the Lord sends rain on the earth" (1 Kings 17:14). And the meal and the oil did not fail. But the Bible does not say that meal and oil materialized out of nothing while somebody was watching. The action of a miracle is more mysterious than that.

Elijah's successor, Elisha, removed the effects of a poison gourd from a pot of stew to feed a company of prophets sitting before him. We can do that nowadays, perhaps, by steam distillation, but at that time it was said to be a miracle. Elisha also "multiplied" some loaves of bread to go with the stew.

> A man came from Baal-shalishah, bringing food from the first fruits to the man of God: twenty loaves of barley, and fresh ears of grain in his sack. Elisha said, "Give it to the people and let them eat." But his servant said, "How can I set this before a hundred people?" So he repeated, "Give it to the people and let them eat, for thus says the Lord 'They shall eat and have some left.'" He set it before them, they ate and had some left, according to the word of the Lord. 2 Kings 4:42-44

Twenty loaves apparently fed one hundred people. How is not clear.

These miracles reinforce again and again the simple message that God will provide bread for those with faith in him. They also serve another purpose—to validate Jesus's later miracles with authority from the past. If it were the only miracle ever performed in human history, Jesus's miracle of the loaves and fishes would prompt a sense of wonder, but also, perhaps, a deep skepticism. It is more easily digested by his friends when it is part of a tradition of bread miracles like Elisha's and the manna marvel. The past has powerful authority in the present. Tradition's value is that it can satisfy our need for continuity and normalcy and protect us from the febrile stress of youthful revolution. In Scripture, the familiarity of the bread miracles by the time Jesus arrives on the scene acts as a stabilizing counterweight to the awe that each of Jesus's miracles evokes, and allows us to digest them without spiritual dyspepsia. By the time Jesus performs his astonishing deeds, it's clear that bread miracles form part of God's plan and are as common as water.

Bread in the New Testament

Jesus's miracles always seem to have a magical quality, but they are never hollowly spectacular. They rescue people from disease or hunger, or they extend kindness to lonely or unhappy people. They are always life-giving and play out God the Father's strategy of divine solicitude for his children. These miracles also illuminate momentous truths.

In the miracle of the loaves and fishes, Jesus provides food for thousands of his followers—people who had honored him by sitting still while he delivered his teaching.

> As he went ashore, he saw a great crowd; and he had compassion for them, because they were like sheep without a shepherd; and he began to teach them many things. When it grew late, his disciples came to him and said, "This is a deserted place and the hour is now very late, send them away so that they may go into the surrounding country and villages and buy something for themselves to eat." But he answered them, "You give them something to eat." They said to him, "Are we to go out and buy two hundred denarii worth of bread, and give it to them to eat?" And he said to them, "How many loaves have you? Go and see." When they had found out, they said, "Five and two fish." Then he ordered them to get all the people to sit down in groups on the green grass. So they sat down in groups of hundreds and of fifties. Taking the five loaves and the two fish, he looked up to heaven and blessed and broke the loaves, and gave them to his disciples to set before the people, and he divided the two fish among them all. And all ate and were filled; and they took up twelve baskets full of broken pieces and of the fish. Those who had eaten the loaves numbered five thousand men.
> Mark 6:34-44

What do we learn from this miracle in the twenty-first century? If you pass up a meal to pray or to listen to God's word or to advance another person's well-being, God the Father will take care of you. Fair's fair, after all, especially in the court of heaven. It's also clear that there are no limits to

God's solicitude for his friends, or his friends-to-be. If he can stretch five loaves and two fishes to feed five thousand men, then he can feed the whole world with a strawberry patch. After the loaves and fishes miracle, the question of God's providing can no longer be in doubt for people of faith.

Finally, it's made clear again that "Give us this day our daily bread" asks for more than loaves. What Jesus fed these people was almost a full meal, even by modern standards. Nutritionists might quibble that two food groups were missing—fruit and vegetables—but in those days bread was much more nourishing than it is today. Jesus's miracles clearly tell us that "our daily bread" means at the very least a square meal, but all kinds of other solicitude as well.

Peter and the Coin

Jesus gives the impression, once in a while, that his miracles (based on faith) are little more than the easy tricks of a practiced conjuror who can pull rabbits out of top hats or elephants from behind empty curtains on cue. He even mocks his audience's skepticism now and then with an especially extravagant magical flourish that challenges the spectators to scratch their heads and try to figure out what's going on. On one occasion, Jesus tells Peter to go and pull a coin out of one of the fish in the sea.

> When they reached Capernaum, the collectors of the temple tax came to Peter and said, "Does your teacher not pay the temple tax?" He said "Yes, he does." And when he came home, Jesus spoke of it first, asking, "What do you think Simon? From whom do kings of the earth take toll or tribute? From their children or from others?" When Peter said "From others," Jesus said to him, "Then the children are free. However, so that we do not give offense to them, go to the sea and cast a hook; take the first fish that comes up; and when you open its mouth, you will find a coin; take that and give it to them for you and me." Matthew 17:24-27

What a delightful story for the child in every one of us! How much more entertaining than the trite mysteries of the party magicians or Uncle Harry's juggling. This coin miracle also scorns weighty books of theological analysis and leaves them behind in our imagination. What this miracle evokes is the childish fun of flying kites and the mystery of sailing little boats that don't sink in the park's pond. This coin miracle is the stuff of fantasy come true. But it still delivers buckets of truth. Money is necessary of course, it says, but a person should never fret about it. With faith, all the money that's needed will appear.

It is astonishing to discover that God the Father and Jesus become powerless where there is no faith, and no desire to know God.

> He came to his hometown and began to teach the people in their synagogue, so that they were astounded and said, "Where did this man get this wisdom and these deeds of power? Is not this the carpenter's son? Is not his mother called Mary? And are not his brothers James and Joseph and Simon and Judas? And are not all his sisters with us? Where then did this man get all this?" And they took offense at him. But Jesus said to them, "Prophets are not without honor except in their own country and in their own house." And he did not do many deeds of power there, because of their unbelief. Matthew 13:54-58

Jesus lost his powers, it seems. God can turn a catfish into a cantaloupe, where there is faith. What is really hard for God the Father to accomplish is a conversion of the stubborn human heart, because he will never overrule it.

The Fourth Petition Word by Word: *Give*

The word *give* in "Give us ... bread" is carefully chosen. The petition does not say: "With respect, your majesty, some of your people are hungry, and we rely as always on your magnanimity to provide them with the bread that they need." That would be the proper way to speak to the King of kings, the one who has been greatly honored a moment ago in "Thy kingdom come." But "Give us ... bread" doesn't connect with "Thy kingdom come," it harks back to the head of the prayer and says "Father ... Give us bread." That's because providing bread is the role of a dad or a mom, not a king. The petition is also careful not to say "Father, pay us the bread that we have earned," because we have earned nothing and have no wages due. Equally the petition does not say, "Father, *please* give us bread," because we are children, and young children often do not say "Please" to their father. Children know their father will feed them, which is a kind of faith. In fact, they would be dumbstruck if he stopped. The Father himself doesn't expect "Please," either. He acknowledges his obligations and doles out bread and butter without chattering about it. What the prayer has done at this point is force the person praying into the correct spiritual posture—that of a little child with faith in his father's (or his mother's) providing. "Whoever becomes humble like this child, is the greatest in the kingdom of heaven" (Matthew 18:4).

"Give" also implies a second word standing before it, but unspoken: "Father, *you* give us this day our daily bread. Our own talents cannot secure it." The person praying is putting his life in order. He promises not to spend his energies grubbing around for a living for himself and his dependents. Instead, he relies on God the Father to care for him and pursues higher spiritual values. He knows at last that a young child's faith in his father is never in vain.

> "Ask, and it will be given you; search, and you will find; knock, and the door will be opened for you. For everyone who asks receives, and everybody who searches finds, and for everyone who knocks, the door will be opened. Is there any one among you who, if your child asks for bread, will give him a stone? Or if the child asks for a fish, will give a snake? If you then, who are evil, know how to give good gifts to your children, how much more will your Father in heaven give good things to those who ask him?"
> Matthew 7:7-11

The Fourth Petition Word by Word: *Us*

Jesus's prayer provides no place for the insertion of personal requests, even of the most unselfish kind: "Please cure my father of cancer. Please make my depressed sister happy." The reason seems to be this: "Your Father knows what you need before you ask him" (Matthew 6:8). The prayer's purpose is not to extract from the deity the things we want, such as our mother's pension. It is to cultivate the faith that gives the Father a free hand in providing what he knows we really need for ourselves, and for the community at large.

In almost every person there is a tendency toward solitude, a cold rejection of society. Other people are a nuisance, a source of irritation, or a risk of hostility. So we avoid them. We do cultivate a few friends, but not many, considering all the wonderful potential friends that we have all around us. If we are religious, we try to penetrate the veils of contemplation, or assiduously search Holy Scripture for deeper meanings, or attend religious services more often in an attempt to be good and holy. But Jesus says through this one eloquent word, *us,* that there is more to loving God than all that religious stuff. Each person is embedded in God's community and we are called to orient life toward that truth. "Give us ... bread" says this: "We pray as a community for your care. And when one of us receives bread—which always comes from you—he or she will share it generously with all the rest." This is the acid test of the conscience, the concrete footing of religion, the intended outcome of the love of God and neighbor.

Jesus delivers a terrible warning to the antisocial recluse that his stubborn solitude can become eternal. But read closely. The warning is wrapped in a promise and an opportunity as well.

> When the Son of Man comes in his glory, and all the angels with him, then he will sit on the throne of his glory. All the nations will be gathered before him, and he will separate people from one another, as a shepherd separates the sheep from the goats; and he will put the sheep at his right hand, and the goats at the left. Then the king will say to those at his right hand, "Come, you that are blessed by my father, inherit the kingdom prepared for you from the foundation of the world, for I was hungry and you gave me food, I was thirsty and you gave me something to drink. I was a stranger and you welcomed me, I was naked and you gave me clothing, I was sick and you took care of me, I was in prison and you visited me." Then the righteous will answer him, "Lord, when was it that we saw you hungry, and gave you food, or thirsty and gave you something to drink? And when was it that we saw you a stranger and welcomed you, or naked and gave you clothing? And when was it that we saw you sick or in prison and visited you?" And the king will answer them, "Truly, I tell you just as you did it to one of the least of these who are members of my family, you did it to me." Then he will say to those at his left hand, "You that are accursed, depart from me into the eternal fire prepared for the devil and his angels; for I was hungry, and you gave me no food, I was thirsty, and you gave me nothing to drink, I was a stranger and you did not welcome me, naked, and you did not give me clothing, sick and in prison, and you did not visit me." Then they will also answer, "Lord when was it that we saw you hungry, or thirsty, or a stranger, or naked, or sick, or in prison, and did not take care of you?" Then he will answer them, "Truly I tell you, just as you did not do it to one of the least of these, you did not do it to me." And these will go away into eternal punishment, but the righteous into eternal life. Matthew 25:31-46

This grave duty to share our bread with others prompted Jesus to compare a rich man trying to get into heaven with a camel trying to squeeze through the eye of a needle. In other words, it's impossible for a man to get through the narrow gate bloated with riches. Only pencil-thin philanthropists will succeed in getting through into the paradise beyond the needle's eye.

Sitting on wealth is one of the greatest crimes against the kingdom. It robs other people of the bread that God gives the whole community and intends us to share. This issue is not only spiritual, it is also political. A man who hoards wealth rejects the authority of the king who gave up bread and everything else for humankind. The rich man positions himself outside the kingdom of God by nothing less than an act of treason.

A person must always act in the community's best interests because he is, in fact, the property of the community—not in the sense of a serf or a slave or a bondsman, but in the sense that God loves him both individually and through the community, where God the Father dwells in love. Paul puts it this way: a person is not free to do what he wishes, even with his own body, because he has been "bought with a price—the death of Jesus" (1 Corinthians 6:20), who died for the whole of humankind. The truth is that we now belong to Jesus through the community, and he belongs to us by his act of love.

The paradox of love is that it binds not only the person who receives kindness, but also the person who does the giving. He, too, becomes a bondsman of love. This point is brought out by a passage in *The Grey Seas Under,* a book by Canadian author Farley Mowat. It tells the true story of *Foundation Franklin,* an ocean-going tug that was owned by the Foundation Co. of Canada, a construction company based in Montreal. In its early years, *Foundation Franklin* had difficulty getting contracts to salvage wrecks at sea because it was not known to the seafaring community of eastern Canada. One day there was a terrible accident among a group of people fishing on the ice floes off Newfoundland. Without thought of payment, *Foundation Franklin* and other ships rushed to the rescue of the people on the ice. From that day on, Mowat writes, the people of the outports of Newfoundland claimed *Foundation Franklin* as their own. "From the hour that she landed her cargo of survivors at St. John's, she ceased to be a foreign vessel—now she belonged to the islanders—and they to her," Mowat wrote.[9] The ship's crew were always free to come and go, and do what they wished with the ship, but they had bound themselves to the people with an act of love and would never escape into solitude again.

That's why Jesus's prayer says "Give *us*... bread." All the bread that's available, here and there, is for sharing, in love. Like it or not, each person is tied to the community with the iron bonds of love created by what he has given to the community himself, by what he has received back from the community, and by what comes to us all from God. Each person belongs to the community in love. It is a criminal act of solitude to pray "Give *me* my daily bread."

The Fourth Petition Word by Word: *This Day*

The kingdom has many doors, and many locks that keep people out. One of these locks is anxiety. It kills joy in the simple things of life, stops the celebration of friendship, and damages health. When the future arrives, anxiety leaves behind a life that has hardly been lived. Jesus's prayer asks for only enough bread for twenty-four hours—this one day. In this light, a person's career, his mortgages, and his children's education all cease to be causes of worry. They are not treated lightly, of course, but provision for them is made and then the risks are forgotten. "So do not worry about tomorrow, for tomorrow will bring worries of its own. Today's trouble is enough for today" (Matthew 6:34).

In asking only for this day's bread, our view of the future changes from the expectation of a dreaded burden to an exciting adventure in faith. The Father to whom we entrust our future is that same infinite being who made the sun and the stars and orchestrated the majesty of all the ages. His allotted task is simple: to provide the individual's and the community's needs for twenty-four hours. The prayer whispers *sotto voce:* "Can there be any need to worry? Our problems are now in the hands of a person who demonstrated his capacity to handle them billions of years ago."

We know, of course, that God the Father does not seem to always remember human needs. Children do have accidents. Promotions are missed. Mortgages can't be paid. That's when "Give us *this day*...bread" works at its deepest levels. It says to God: "Look, we have to ask for something, we're only flesh and blood after all, but we'll make it very little, just the basic food for today. For the rest we'll accept whatever you send, even if it's not what we think we want. You always know what's best." The person is now free to be happy, hour by hour, day by day, and enjoy whatever beauty there may still be left in life, even in the midst of his suffering—but not the suffering of anxiety.

The prayer becomes a hymn of mystical freedom, an abandonment to God's will, and a rejection of the imprisoning concerns of the self. "Give us *this* day...bread" is also a confession. It comes after a prayer that the kingdom will come, which can only mean that the community must still be alienated from the king. The two words "this day" add this idea: "Look after us Father, even today, when we have alienated ourselves from you, the one person who deeply cares about us." When we say this through the words "this day," we are staring right ahead at the coming of the kingdom: God the Father caring for humans, while they all overcome their alienation together.

The Fourth Petition Word by Word: *Our Daily Bread*

The order of Jesus's petitions is edifying: "Father,...Thy kingdom come, Give us this day our daily bread." We ask for bread only after we have centered our spirit on God and tilled the ground of our soul until it is ready to grow a harvest of faith that God the Father will indeed supply us with our daily bread. That's why Jesus's bread stands for more than bread on the table, more even than enough food in the larder to keep us nourished. This most basic of nourishment, bread, stands for a simple life that is founded on faith in God's providing, rather than on the security of the food chain.

Bread is used as a symbol for many spiritual values in Scripture. In fact, bread is probably the most commonly used and the most multifaceted symbol in the whole of Scripture, old and new. The ancient Hebrews, for example, always had a golden table laden with "the bread of the presence" (Exodus 25:30), which was their welcome to God as a guest and marked his presence amongst them. God doesn't eat, so the bread was consumed by the priests (Leviticus 24:5-9).

In the New Testament, Jesus uses bread as a dynamic sign, shifting it from one meaning to another, even within the same passage. On one occasion, he interprets bread as a symbol of arrogant self-reliance and a lack of faith in God the Father.

> Then Jesus was led up by the Spirit into the wilderness to be tempted by the devil. He fasted forty days and forty nights, and afterwards he was famished. The tempter came and said to him, "If you are the Son of God, command these stones to become loaves of bread." But he answered, "It is written, one does not live by bread alone; but by every word that comes from the mouth of God." Matthew 4:1-4

This episode turns bread as a symbol of the spiritual life on its head. The tempter wants Jesus to abandon his faith in God the Father and rely on his own divine powers to make bread for himself alone. Here, bread represents an inward-turning egotism, an obsession with one's own needs. Jesus refuses to use his power in solitude, even though he is hungry after forty days of fasting. He will rely on his faith in God the Father for bread, and in doing so, restore bread to its symbolic connection with faith.

In this dark drama with the tempter, Jesus condemns both the rich and the poor in one blow. The rich employ their wealth to gain personal advantage outside the community—the sin of arrogance. Jesus denounces these people by refusing to use his own powers in the way that they do to obtain loaves of bread only for himself. But the poor are also chastised here. In this context, the poor are those people who nurse the conviction that they are alone and powerless, left by God the Father to fend for themselves. These forlorn people would jump at the chance of free food provided by the tempter and would gobble up his ill-gotten bread just to stay safe. The poor commit the crime of anxiety, which causes all their attention to be focused on their material needs, as the tempter expected Jesus to do. The poor and the rich are the same kinds of people. The attitude that underlies both spiritual defects is materialism, which is focused on the bread rather than on the divine provider. Jesus gives up his chance at the tempter's bread in order to place his faith in the solicitude of God the Father.

A real friend of God's is neither powerful in his own right by means of his riches, nor powerless within the embrace of God the Father. Impotence is only an illusion thrown up by spiritual pessimism. A friend of God's always knows that bread will be provided as a response to his faith. This is real power, a spiritual force that comes not from the individual, but to the individual from God the Father. But the blessings that this faith in God the Father brings are not for the individual alone. They are always for him and for the whole community together.

Jesus also makes bread a symbol of the wholeness of humanity—the perfect harmony of a healthy, well-nourished body and a robust soul living in faith together. In fact, bread becomes a symbol of Jesus himself, the most perfect human being, the Son of Man. Jesus was not only perfect because of his luminous spirituality. He was perfect because of the full breadth of his profound humanity, which was the unity of all the spiritual and corporeal dimensions of his way of life.

"Do not work for the food that perishes, but for the food that endures for eternal life, which the Son of Man will give you. For it is on him that God, the Father, has set his seal." Then they said to him, "What must we do to perform the works of God?" Jesus answered them, "This is the work of God, that you believe in him whom he has sent." So they said to him, "What sign are you going to give us then so that we may see it and believe you? What work are you performing? Our ancestors ate the manna in the wilderness; as it is written: 'He gave them bread from heaven to eat.'" Then Jesus said to them, "Very truly, I tell you, it was not Moses who gave you the bread from heaven, but it is my Father who gives you the true bread from heaven. For the bread of God is that which comes down from heaven and gives life to the world." They said to him "Sir, give us this bread, always." Jesus said to them "I am the bread of life. Whoever comes to me will never be hungry and whoever believes in me will never be thirsty." John 6:27-35

Here, the title Bread of Life becomes a partner to Jesus's other appelation, the Son of Man. Both epithets identify a perfect, triumphant humanity within Jesus, a humanity that is crippled and imprisoned within all other people, but can still be healed and liberated to some extent. An individual cannot become divine like Jesus, but in the perfection of faith, he can become more human like Jesus. And he can do so by receiving the bread of life within him. "I am the living bread that came down from heaven. Whoever eats of this bread will live forever and the bread that I will give for the life of the world is my flesh" (John 6:51). Jesus is even more specific at the Last Supper. "While they were eating, Jesus took a loaf of bread, and after blessing it, he broke it, gave it to the disciples, and said, 'Take, eat; this is my body'" (Matthew 26:26-28). To eat the consecrated bread of the Eucharist is to receive Jesus, the bread of life, into our souls. This is the most complete union of two persons possible—the union of the whole of the humanity and the divinity of Jesus with the whole of the communicant, body and spirit.

So what range of breads does "Give us this day our daily bread" pray for? It prays for groceries for the individual and the community, all shared together, in a simple life. It also prays for a fuller humanity through the nourishment provided by faith in God the Father who cares for his children in every possible way.

7

And Forgive Us Our Sins;

We Too Forgive All Those Who Trespass Against Us

Forgiveness is a journey across the frontier between the viper-infested desert of hatred and the soft ascendant meadows of the kingdom of God. Forgiveness is a journey, but it is also a chase—a vigorous hunt for a higher justice that is based not on the balance of crime and compensation but on a commitment to caring for the offender. Forgiveness is the escape from the rancidity of rancor into eternal brotherhood, even with criminals. Forgiveness is a prerequisite for the release, like a dove, of our humanity itself.

In this prayer, the forgiveness that we seek from God does involve a journey—all the way from our acknowledgment of the Fatherhood of an offended God to the act of asking him to reconcile us with himself. "Father, ... Forgive us." But there's more than divine forgiveness involved in this trip. There's the forgiveness of each person for the other, and that is more than a journey—it is a prerequisite of the coming of the kingdom.

To Forgive

The word *forgive* is one of a family of English words that use the prefix *for(e)*. To forgive carries the sense of beforehand giving, which suggests the damaged relationship is healed by the injured party reaching out to the criminal, before seeking any compensation. To forgive is to wipe the slate clean. With many ifs and buts, we can say that to forgive is to forget an injury and not allow it to influence one's generosity to the offender. But forgiving is not sentimental. It is never a fervid rush of feeling that wipes the slate clean. Forgiving is forgetting, but the forgetting is based on the deepest wisdom. Forgiving must be mutual in its intent and deeply caring in its policy, renewing both the victim and the criminal together. Still, anything less wise than forgetting is not forgiving.

Everybody suffers injuries from time to time—the individual, society at large, and God himself. The response of each of these persons to an injury depends on many things, such as the victim's power, the criminal's mindset, and considerations of mercy and rehabilitation.

Law-abiding individuals are powerless to punish a tormentor, because society insists we never take retribution into our own hands. Thus thwarted, we resort to petty revenge, such as blackening the offender's name or nursing hatred within our hearts. We do this because we have been made to appear weak. We were tricked by a con man or beaten by a thug. And our dignity has been assaulted. And that is the deepest cut of all—a wound to one's pride. We may also have lost something valuable, such as wealth or good health, which we want restored in full. After all this injury, we ache to hit back. But the law-abiding citizen always abdicates this lust for justice to a higher power.

This higher power, the society in which we live, rarely forgives a crime by forgetting it, at least, not until the criminal has been made to pay a price, and often not even then. There are sound reasons for this tit-for-tat justice. We can never read a criminal's mind, and we don't know if he will commit the crime again. By punishing all criminals every time they offend, we try to ensure that none of them repeats the crime, whatever his mindset. Punishing the actual criminal also deters any tendency to felony in potential criminals who may be drawn to the pleasures of the same wrongdoing. But the reason for punishing lawbreakers runs deeper even than that. Society is not only harmed by crime in a concrete way through physical damage to its citizens, crime also dishonors society's most cherished values. If a man murders another man's son and is allowed to get off scot-free, the son's life and all human life has been cheapened and the father's grief has been trampled. To forgive a crime without any punishment is childishly romantic. What is needed in the justice system is not the raucous rubbish of lofty forgiveness ideals. It is the cleansing of crime out of the bowels of society. At least that's the way many of us think.

God the Father, the highest power of all, also seeks a cleansing of society. But he makes use of radical forgiveness and forgetting, instead of onerous correction. God the Father has a right to choose between punishment and forgiveness because he is a victim himself. He is injured deeply by any offense committed against one of his children. And sometimes he is insulted by crimes that are entirely solitary, such as drug abuse and self-indulgence—crimes against this particular beloved child of the Father. But he does not respond with resentment or with punishment or by cultivating a pained distance. He pays off the debt himself through the sacrifice of his Son, and he courts the criminal—even seduces him—with a Father's love and humility. Far from being childishly romantic, this approach is much more effective than society's approach, because God the Father looks at the problem more deeply. His thinking runs beyond human insight to reveal vast new territories of criminology that would have been hard to explore without God's own example as the pioneer.

How God Courts Our Friendship

The petition that partners "And forgive us our sins" is "Hallowed be thy name." These two petitions together form one holistic spiritual unit and unveil the second person of the Trinity—the High Priest, who reconciles us with God the Father. Thus, it is God himself who jump-starts the process of reconciliation, first by inspiring us to pray Jesus's prayer, "Hallowed be thy name," and then, through that prayer, by inspiring us to honor God the Father and all his creation as penitent people looking for friendship. After this job has been done, we can say "Forgive us our sins," and reconciliation is completed by God's decision to forgive us. To understand this process, we must look at both petitions closely.

The first particle, "Hallowed be thy name," asks God to help all people in the world recognize that God and his creation are holy. This old English word *holy* means that the world we live in is not only a thing of beauty. It is whole and wholesome, free from flaw, and sacred, because it issues from the Creator. "Hallowed be thy name" points directly at one of the ways in which God tries to court us into giving him our love—through the sacred beauty of the natural world. "There must be a God," some people say, "because there are butterflies (or rainbows or roses)." Who hasn't felt an urge to reform his life while standing on a cliff in the rain watching the timeless sea break on the immutable cliffs? "Forgive us our sins," we might say, overcome with awe as we watch the rain-pelted majesty of the waves moving rhythmically to a greater power. "He washed his soul in the west wind, And his body in the sea," G. K. Chesterton says of King Alfred standing on a thrusting spit in *The Ballad of the White Horse*.[1] God works on our spirits partly through the cleansing wonders of nature. But how?

The Divine Seduction of Butterflies

The three fundamentals of the universe—space-time, energy, and natural law—are all seamlessly simple, and as far as we know, the same here and in the Crab Nebula, one million light-years away. Natural laws are also the same here and that far away. Energy is an identical substance in both places. And the nature of space-time means it is the same all the way from here to over there, and all the way from back then until right now. Mysteriously, though, these three ultrasimple things work together to create enormous variety. The uncountable stars are all different from one another, and each changes all the time. The number of wood lice is in the hundreds of millions, and in an aeon or two, wood lice may evolve into centipedes or something else as yet unimagined. And every single wood louse version will be distinct from all the others.

The three fundamentals of the universe combine in billions of ways to produce a colossal engine of creativity. But they are not the only elements within the things of nature. There is also character, design, and artistry. The daytime sky, which reaches all the way up to the stars, does not appear to be a vaulting void. It radiates an intense blue that expresses distance to the human eye, as if an artist had laid down a counterpoint between the sky's blue and the greens and browns of the earth, which are closer to the observer and more "bottomed." The polar night is lit by the aurora borealis, as if a painter had donated a work of chiaroscuro to people starved of sunlight. The aurora is so beautiful, one tribe of native people calls its magical, drifting lights "the souls of people yet to be born." In the world of living things, the supposedly impersonal process of evolution has given us a menagerie of fantastic creatures—elephants that speak a language we can't hear, hippopotamuses that mourn the death of other animals, fearless mice, thousands of fantastic beetles, minute but unconquerable viruses, a living green carpet on the earth to walk upon, and fine animal companions wherever we go.

The beauty of God's creation is found everywhere we have been and everywhere we haven't, as we soon discover when we go exploring. And the world's beauty always engages the human spirit with joy. A priceless spectacle may come and go in a moment, such as the sliding and lurching of a leaf falling from a tree in autumn, on a bright day, leaving an enchanted soul. Or the same show may be repeated for aeons, such as the setting sun, until even the most sensitive imagination tends to be bored. G. K. Chesterton says such fatigue is purely human:

> It may not be automatic necessity that makes all daisies alike; it may be that God makes every daisy separately, but has never got tired of making them. It may be that he has the eternal appetite of infancy; for we have sinned and grown old, and our Father is younger than we. The repetition in Nature may not be a mere recurrence; it may be a theatrical encore.[2]

Rabindranath Tagore says in *Gitanjali*, "When I go from hence, let this be my parting word, that what I have seen is unsurpassable.... In this playhouse of infinite forms I have had my play and here have I caught sight of him that is formless."[3]

The cosmic imagination is not just artistic, it is deadly serious in its determination to renew and refresh. That's why its beauty always favors the creation of new life. When plants are ready to reproduce, they make lovely flowers to attract the bees. It's doubtful the bees can appreciate the flowers' beauty. Birds about to mate do not just pass a signal, they display their most magnificent plumage, like the peacock, or strut on a mysterious stage, like Japanese cranes and Prairie grouse. Humans are most lovely in their childbearing years. As they get older, their beauty loses its luminosity. Clearly, the divine artist favors love, birth, and inner renewal.

The world's beauty may be joyful like the peacock's tail, stern like the dark majesty of a tornado, playful like a kitten, or even tragic like the dying swan, but it is always moral, because it is never showy for its own sake. Beauty is inexorably linked to function—any part of a living creature that is not used is lost, no matter how beautiful it may be. The eyes of cave dwellers atrophy and go blind, and in later generations disappear all together because they do not function in darkness. Paralyzed human legs, even the most shapely, lose their elegance and their capacity to walk. This iron rule of "use it or lose it" is not fully explained by the theory of evolution, which often misses the point of what we really want to know about the natural world. But we cannot escape the conclusion that "use it or lose it" is part of the self-discipline and the integrity of the divine artist. It invites us to examine our own integrity, or lack of it.

The Creator's imagination is not only playful and moral, it is also political. The celestial painter always creates beauty that delights the openhearted, the poor, and the simple, rather than the wealthy, who already have their lesser but more controllable comforts. The ageless diamonds of the rich are never as lovely as the beads of dew that disappear in the morning sun before they can be collected, and enchant the hungry peasant walking to the fields. Gold may be the hinge of mighty kingdoms and the bedrock of great currencies, but it is never as commanding as the living dandelions that grow on a lawn, tantalizing the householder with a gold he cannot eradicate and a beautiful flower he may pick but cannot keep. The portraits on a rich man's wall are never as inspiring as the nobility of a human companion engaged in kindly work.

The divine artist reveals his beauty most fully, and most shyly, to those people who try hard to be his friends. And the more they revere him and cast off the burden of wealth, the more beautiful the natural world becomes. It may offer them a vision of ageless majesty for a split second in the changing shapes of a towering cloud, or present a hint of fearless dignity in the wind-carved cast of an iceberg, which can conjure up stirring memories of pride and conquest that cannot quite be recalled. God is always a politician, because winning friends is the strategy of all politicians, good or bad.

The sublime beauty of the natural world is an invitation to all God's children to throw away their obsession with their appetites in favor of entering into the joy of the Father's creation, and going from there into his kingdom, absolved of sin. That's what the prayer "Hallowed be thy name" reveals: a God who tries to win over his children with the finest of gifts, despite their rage and self-indulgence, a God who is always hoping his people will become reconciled to him by hallowing his name and his creation. The particle "Hallowed be thy name" reveals a God who wants to charm us into love so that he can forgive us, as in the second part of this spiritual unit, "Forgive us our sins."

How Are We Forgiven?

If we think hard about "Forgive us our sins" in the light of civil justice and the revelations of Scripture, we are forced to conclude that God must receive some compensation or makeweight for our crimes when he forgives us. We can't just intone the words *Forgive us* and Bingo! we are reconciled with the Creator. The gospels tell us that God's act of restitution to God the Father is performed by Jesus, the Son of God and the Son of Man, the one who embodies the best of our humanity within his sublime divinity. And what a restitution Jesus makes! The sheer breadth of his suffering on the cross makes his sacrifice an act of penal genius.

Jesus suffered all the kinds of human torment one could imagine to make compensation to God the Father for all the crimes that human beings commit. We wound people with calumnies—Jesus is mocked by the soldiers over his claims to divinity, an alleged falsehood. We stab a stranger in the street with a knife—Jesus is flogged with a scourge with metal tips. We steal—Jesus gives up everything he has. We rape—Jesus is pierced with the lance. We abuse our authority and play God—Jesus gives up all his divine power and allows himself to be humiliated on a wooden monument of shame. We hate those who should be our friends—Jesus loves even his enemies. We strut around puffed up with pride—Jesus endures the humiliation of a seeming failure in his mission as spiritual leader. We abandon people in trouble—Jesus stands in solidarity with them in his own abandonment. We commit murder—Jesus gives up his life. And finally, Jesus dies for the truth that he came to teach. This truth that has been denied by our crimes has been reasserted in advance, so that there can never be any doubt. His sacrifice is the direct opposite of the crime.

Jesus's sacrifice accomplishes more than just our forgiveness. It accomplishes the complete rehabilitation of the criminal. That's why it is called redemption, which means rescue from alienation. And this rescue is as free as the air and the sun and the sand. You just grab a piece of it for yourself any time you like.

What the criminal is saved from is the spiritual fallout of his crimes, especially the terrible punishments he inflicts upon himself. In the secret knowledge of his crime, the criminal mutilates his inner self by alienating himself from the love of God and from the love of his friends (though a diluted secondhand companionship with other people may still survive). The criminal also alienates himself from the love of himself by lowering his self-esteem, catastrophically. This is true even of the most hardened criminals, although most would never admit it. Joseph Stalin, the twentieth century Russian tyrant, tried to husband his self-respect by forbidding his minions to give him details of the suffering of his victims. Stalin knew only too well that too much knowledge of his victims' agonies might weaken his resolve. Mafia dons in Sicily beat up local people who do not treat them as men of respect, precisely because the dons know that they do not deserve that respect and must gain the appearance of it by force. A person confident in his integrity does not terrorize others into acknowledging it. A con man in Toronto cheats a friend out of a large sum of money and blames the friend for being so foolish as to trust him. That's surely self-recognition of the con man's base nature.

Human nature is the same in every person. What distinguishes the criminal is his willingness to devalue his self-esteem in return for financial or other gain, and to compensate with a phony pride based on some hollow value such as machismo or bravado. Deep down, though, the criminal always knows the truth.

Knowing their own debasement so well, the guilty feel obliged, if only beyond their consciousness, to impose a punishment upon themselves for this loss of self-respect. And some do, in the most exotic ways. They mutilate themselves or do drugs or experiment with despair. But this need to punish one's self is always satisfied by the agonies of Jesus, who suffers on the criminal's behalf, with great love. Jesus's suffering is more extreme than any punishment any person could possibly inflict upon himself. Therefore, the account is closed, for even the most despicable criminal who can, if he will accept rescue, hold his head high again as if nothing had happened. The criminal's crime has been paid for in full by a most awesome penalty—the capital punishment of the King.

The King is executed, not the criminal, because this is a matter of the highest royal policy. It is the King's own wish. And it is his royal prerogative. He will brook no argument, and who can gainsay him? This is also the will of a father rescuing his children. He rushes into burning buildings or swims out into a stormy sea or leaps in front of a bullet. He gives everything for his children, even, if necessary, his own life. This divine Father gives something even closer to his heart than his own life—the life of his Son. In the light of this iron determination by the Creator himself to rescue us, our own shame becomes irrelevant, once we accept the divine rescue. We have little choice but to yield graciously to the policies of a higher power and accept freedom from our inner degradation. But redemption's healing goes further even than that. The criminal is not only rescued from himself. By accepting death willingly, on our behalf, Jesus reinstates the criminal, guiltless, before God the Father and the King and everybody else. Crimes are not only forgiven, they are utterly forgotten.

Everybody is forgiven all at once, again and again, as long as they want forgiveness and are ready to start again, even if they have already started again one hundred times, and failed. God the Father refuses to consider the danger of recidivism, one that so frightens the civil society in which we live. God the Father cares even less about any loss of his own personal dignity as a result of his being taken for granted, again and again. He opts for the most radical forgiveness—before the crime has even been committed. The only condition is that the criminal repents and embraces reform every single time that he seeks forgiveness. But he can fail the first time and the seventy-seventh time and rescue is still there, waiting for him to pick himself up off the floor and totter forward again for a few steps. This message is absolutely clear. "Be on your guard! If another disciple sins, you must rebuke the offender, and if there is repentance you must forgive. And if the same person sins against you seven times a day and turns back to you seven times and says 'I repent,' you must forgive" (Luke 17:3-4). This flood tide of forgiveness is unstoppable and keeps washing society clean, again and again.

We Too Forgive Others

Jesus's prayer can be mined for treasures deeper and deeper, apparently without end. But which version do we quarry—the Aramaic original that Jesus spoke, the Greek of the evangelists, or the prayers spoken today in modern languages? We can't go back to the Aramaic. That has been lost. So scholars feel they are going to the prayer's source by studying the ancient Greek. But that is not the original either. It has already been "developed" by the evangelists. Matthew has added bits and pieces here and there. Luke has maintained the original number of petitions, but the wording, in some cases, is further from Jesus's original than the same petitions in Matthew, we are told. Besides, the prayer that is sacred to people today is not the Aramaic or the Greek. It is the version they pray in French or Maltese or Swahili. Most people know nothing of the originals. And if scholars squeezed some new meaning out of the Greek, it's unlikely the prayer spoken in Berlin or New York would ever be changed. Is this a betrayal of Jesus's intentions? No! All interpretations of Jesus's prayer can be true. The true prayer is what we say daily with devotion, not the words in some other tongue written long ago.

What we look for is not new ideas taken out of this or that version, but the spiritual wisdom found both in the prayer and in other parts of Jesus's teaching. And that can be sought in any translation. If we look at the English, for example, we quickly notice that the petition that begins "Forgive us" is subtly different in Matthew and Luke. The two versions manage to convey two seemingly conflicting ideas of divine forgiveness, which are both authentic at the same time. One lesson is that we must forgive others before God will forgive us. The other is that God forgives us first, before we ever forgive others. Each English translation lays emphasis on one or the other of these two realities.

> Matthew: "And forgive us our trespasses as we forgive those who trespass against us."

> Luke: "*And forgive us our sins; we too forgive all those who trespass against us.*"

The differences are slight, yet revealing. In Matthew, the words "forgive us our trespasses *as* we forgive others" seems to say "forgive us *at the same time* as we forgive others" or "forgive us *in the same measure* as we forgive others." The underlying idea here is that God will forgive us *because* we have forgiven others. God's mercy is linked directly to our own forgiveness of our neighbors. This principle is also enunciated elsewhere in Matthew's gospel. "For if you forgive others their trespasses, your heavenly Father will also forgive you; but if you do not forgive others, neither will your Father forgive your trespasses" (Matt 6:14-15). Luke also quotes Jesus putting forward much the same teaching: "Do not judge, and you will not be judged; do not condemn, and you will not be condemned. Forgive, and you will be forgiven; give and it will be given unto you" (Luke 6:37-38).

Luke's version of the prayer shows the other side of the coin. God forgives us, and after that, "we too" forgive others. The person praying is a little child who imitates his father because he is the most powerful influence in the child's life. The father has forgiven the child, and always will. So the child looks to do as the father does and forgives others, because "what Daddy does" must be right. The child practices forgiveness by loving imitation, but it is not something he ever really understands. We don't understand the radical unconditional forgiveness advocated by Jesus, either. We may try to imitate Jesus, but this is usually against what we consider our better nature. But it's true to say we are forgiven first, then we try to forgive by imitation.

This "God forgives first" notion found in Luke is validated by a deep psychological truth. In both hatred and love, a person makes no real distinction between himself and others, at least deep down. He takes whatever opinion he may have of himself and projects it directly onto others. If he truly loves himself, he can love others. If he cannot forgive himself, he is unable to forgive others.

If the criminal is to be converted out of this ugly introverted mindset, he must begin by forgiving himself; then he will be able to forgive others. But how does a person hate himself one day and then forgive himself the next? Clearly, any lightning forgiveness cannot come from within. It must be prompted somehow from outside. And that's what flows from Jesus's willing submission to torture and death on behalf of every single individual. Whatever the criminal has done, the slate is wiped clean by Jesus, if the criminal wishes it and tries to reform. He has been forgiven by God himself first (Who else can hold him to account?). And now he can truly forgive himself and forget his crimes. Once he can forgive himself, he can truly forgive others. That's the correct sequence of events. God forgives us first magnificently, and then we are able to forgive others. That's the idea captured in Luke's prayer. This "prior forgiveness" idea is also true in a historical sense. Jesus rescued us in the year A.D. 30. We commit our crimes in the twenty-first century. The possibility of God's forgiveness comes first, and then we offend.

In Luke, God's forgiveness is not received, as Matthew suggests, in the same measure as the penitent's forgiveness of his neighbor. God's forgiveness comes first and is always far more generous than we can ever match. It is a marvel of grace that we can never fully understand. But Matthew's truth is not to be denied, either. The rescue that was put into place two thousand years ago by Jesus is not available if we don't forgive others. If we don't learn the lesson of forgiveness from God the Father, his forgiveness will dry up.

The Four Stages of Forgiveness

Forgiveness is like a craggy mountain that has handy rock platforms on the way up, and then a few steep slopes covered with a jumble of boulders close to the top. You can travel up the mountain as far as you like, but very few people reach the summit. Some stop one-quarter of the way up, or halfway up, because they like the view outward from that point and feel good about how far up they have traveled by partly forgiving others. They stop and rest, mightily self-satisfied. Some try to go higher but can't figure out a way through the maze of rocks blocking the way ahead. They halt, sit down, and convince themselves it's risky to go any farther. Few people have the courage to travel to the top and practice the radical, thunderclap forgiveness advocated by Jesus.

Forgiveness can be weak or strong, grudging or inspired. A criminal in the United States kills a man's daughter and is captured by the police. The girl's father leaves the issue of justice to the state by refusing to incite a lynch mob, but pressures the prosecutor to drive hard for the death penalty. Little forgiveness there. In fact, the father loses something precious, which if he thought about it, he would try to protect. His rage against the murderer pollutes his grief and his poignant love for his daughter. Rage and sorrow are like oil and water. They do not mix. A more forgiving father endures his grief and makes no attempt to influence the court on the criminal's sentence. He takes the position that his views of the criminal's actions are biased and the criminal has the right to a fair trial. That's the first stage of forgiveness—neutrality toward the criminal when he faces society's sanctions. A more forgiving father petitions the court to be lenient with his daughter's murderer because of the misfortune the criminal has brought upon himself by his crime. After all, a murderer not only murders his victim, he murders his own soul. In pleading for the criminal, the father ennobles his grief and beautifies his love for his dead daughter. The crime becomes the evil, not the criminal. This is the second stage of forgiveness—advocacy for the criminal.

Forgiveness can go much further than that. A story about King Edward the Confessor, possibly a myth, tells how he caught a thief one day in his apartment. He recognized the man as a poverty-stricken serf and loaded him up with even more of the king's belongings, then ushered him out the back door quickly, before the palace guards could arrive and collar him. Such an act represents the third and fourth stages of forgiveness—recognizing the criminal's handicaps, and rescuing him. Many criminals are people damaged by poverty or abuse, hatred or abandonment. They live without hope of ever being valued as worthwhile people. In this story, King Edward tried to find out why the crime was being committed, and then showed sympathy for the criminal. He also rescued the thief by converting the theft into a gift, so that there was no crime committed. He helped the thief get away so that the authorities would not mark the man as a likely criminal and give him trouble later. Edward's actions are close to the radical forgiveness advocated by Jesus:

> But I say to you that listen, Love your enemies, do good to those who hate you, bless those who curse you, pray for those who abuse you. If anyone strikes you on the cheek, offer the other also; and from anyone who takes away your coat do not withhold even your shirt. Give to everyone who begs from you; and if anyone takes away your goods do not ask for them again. Do to others as you would have them do to you. Luke 6:27-31

But hold on; do you turn the other cheek to the street thug, while he is beating you? Do you bless those who rape you, while they are raping you? Or is this Middle Eastern hyperbole, like Jesus's advocacy of self-mutilation? If you sin with your eye, he says, pluck it out. Better to get into the kingdom of God with one eye than not at all. Very few theologians, if any, would advocate self-inflicted eye surgery for Peeping Toms on the basis of this gospel passage. Are we to take the same skeptical view of the radical forgiveness advocated by Jesus, the idea that we should forgive the crime, in some cases *while it is actually being committed against us?*

In fact, this approach can be a powerfully practical solution. It can work to bury the crime and save the perpetrator. In Nebraska in 1991, a Jewish couple, Michael and Julie Weisser, was the target, along with many others, of vilification and threats by Larry Trapp, the state leader of the Ku Klux Klan. Trapp railed against "kikes," "niggers," and "gooks" and made plans to blow up the Weisser's synagogue. His apartment was filled with guns and Nazi paraphernalia, and he was organizing a group of skinheads to commit violence around the neighborhood. The Weissers suspected the hate-monger's vitriol was the external symptom of a deep unhappiness, according to Kathryn Watterson in her book *Not by the Sword*. The Weissers investigated Trapp and discovered he was a half-blind diabetic amputee who was confined to a wheelchair. They phoned him with love and forgiveness and offered to deliver groceries to his apartment. Trapp was moved by their kindness, but continued his public vilification of ethnic minorities. "I'm sorry I [do] that," he said, "[but] I've been talking like that all my life." Michael asked his congregation for prayers for Trapp. They responded. The effect was powerful. Trapp left the Ku Klux Klan and wrote apologies to as many of his victims as he could find. As Trapp's health deteriorated, the Weisser's brought him to live in their home. He died in the bosom of their family on September 6, 1992. The Weisser's radical forgiveness, while the crime was being committed, rescued the criminal.[4]

Jesus not only preached radical forgiveness, he also practiced it himself. "When they came to the place that is called the Skull, they crucified Jesus there with the criminals, one on his right and one on his left. Then Jesus said 'Father forgive them: for they do not know what they are doing'" (Luke 23:33-34). He didn't say "Go lightly with them Father, they don't know what they are doing, but they are certainly committing a lesser crime." He said forgive them. Wipe the slate clean—even while they are doing this thing to me. He practiced the radical forgiveness he advocated so much in his teaching. Obviously his "love your enemies" admonition was not intended as hyperbole.

But how do we apply this radical forgiveness? How do we protect our children and forgive a pedophile at the same time, in the knowledge that pedophiles act as much out of compulsion as they do out of willfulness, and are rarely cured? How do we forgive a stock artist who manipulates the market and destroys the retirement savings of hundreds of people, and won't return the money when caught? How do we forgive Slobodan Milosevic, the tyrant who presided over a Serbian empire of massacre and financial corruption? And yet, it seems, we must forgive these people, or we will not be forgiven ourselves.

We must first recognize that radical forgiveness is not only a spiritual issue—it always exists in a concrete setting, one in which we must defend ourselves against further crime. What we have to do is find a balance between forgiveness and self-defense, one that probably has to be worked out with the criminal himself. Perhaps we forgive the pedophile, but circle him with vigilant friends so that he can't commit the crime again. Perhaps we forgive the habitual rapist, but incarcerate him for his own rehabilitation and for our protection. Is that still forgiveness? If it is, then the issue becomes the quality of the rapist's life in prison and our readiness to admit when the rapist is rehabilitated and release him. The forgetting part of this forgiveness is concern for the rapist's true well-being and a lively readiness to help him return, healed, to a welcoming society.

But is self-defense a factor at all in radical forgiveness? Jesus forgave his enemies while they were in the very act of executing him. Doesn't radical forgiveness ignore personal safety and rely on a lightning strike of love into the criminals' heart, suddenly illuminating for him the dark territory into which he is traveling? That's what Michael and Julie Weisser believed, and it worked. On the other hand, does radical forgiveness always work like that? And is that the real question? Isn't radical forgiveness a powerful prayer for the criminal, without the certainty of a practical solution? These are the questions that trouble us as we try to climb the high mountain peak of forgiveness and scramble through the baffling maze of boulders to reach the top, and there view the world in all its beauty.

Forgiveness is not one act, nor even many. It is a permanent state of mind, or of the heart. Forgiveness is a kind of human liberty, the freedom to be an optimist and to see the good, or at least the potential for good, in other people. Forgiveness is the freedom to be one's true self and to release the wonderful kindness that wants to well up from within. Forgiveness is the freedom to practice a heart-felt sentimentality that is founded on a hard-nosed reality. Forgiveness is one of the limbs of a whole humanity. It is the humble imitation of the innocent child that created the universe and died a terrible death to forgive us, before we had even sinned.

8

And Lead Us Not into Temptation

The psalmist was confident he knew where God leads us, and he rhapsodized about it: "The Lord is my shepherd, I shall not want. He makes me lie down in green pastures; he leads me beside still waters; he restores my soul. He leads me in the right paths for his name's sake" (Psalm 23:1-3). Later, in the New Testament, these lovely pastoral images come to life with Jesus as the shepherd. We are the shepherd's sheep, who are led into the green pastures of the high kingdom. The twenty-third psalm speaks of the sheep's trust in the shepherd: "Even though I walk through the darkest valley, I fear no evil; for you are with me" (Psalm 23:4). Here is the core of this beautiful psalm about God's leadership. Matthew's ending to Jesus's prayer, "But deliver us from evil," echoes these words. The psalm also declares: "He leads me in the right paths for his name's sake." And these words are prophetic of Luke's ending, "And lead us not into temptation."

But Luke's ending raises a question that goes beyond anything found in the twenty-third psalm: Why ever would God lead us into temptation? Many people have asked this puzzling question over the centuries. It's what makes this petition the most enigmatic in the prayer, and perhaps one of the most difficult sentences in Scripture. The problem is not so much theological as it is literary. The things that must be said in Luke's final petition are profound, yet they still must be compressed into six or seven words in keeping with the prayer's powerful brevity. That's why "And lead us not into temptation" needs reflection.

If Jesus's prayer is to keep its brilliant structure as well as its theological depth to the end, this last petition must accomplish several things at once. It must express the actions of a king, because it is partner to "Thy kingdom come." And these two petitions together point to the King as the third person of the Trinity. But the petition "And lead us not into temptation" must also do other things. It must build our faith, because that's what all the second-half petitions do for us. "Give us ... bread" builds our faith in the arrival of our next meal and "Forgive us our sins" builds faith in our reconciliation with the God we have offended. Strange as its language may seem, "And lead us not into temptation" is the only form of this petition that satisfies all the necessary conditions at the same time.

"Father, we will try not to sin" doesn't cut the mustard because it's a promise. All of Jesus's prayer asks God to give us the grace to send our lives in the right direction. None of it is a promise. "We'll try not to sin," would also suggest we can remain loyal to God by ourselves, without divine assistance. "Father, protect us from sin" doesn't work, either. We have the free will to choose virtue or vice. God will not take that away, because when we choose to sin, we use his precious, inalienable gift of free will. That's why God will not protect us from our many decisions to sin in any ironclad way. He will only give us his grace. So we can't say, "And protect us from sin."

"Father, *lead* us not into sin" won't work either, because when we trespass we go it alone. We can't imply that God might lead us into sin in defiance of his own divine wishes. But we have almost arrived at the language we need. This last petition must indeed contain the word *lead*, because it must resonate with "Thy kingdom come," which talks about a king. This King does not rule by applying a straitjacket like Stalin, Hitler, and other tyrant "kings" did to their people. This divine King leads us because this is a democratic kingdom in which we can follow the King, or ignore him, and leave the kingdom at will. So the last petition must contain the request that God lead us. But the petition cannot simply say "And lead us"—end of prayer. It has to say something more, or it is merely a repetition of "Thy kingdom come." But lead us where, and toward what?

The previous two petitions ask God for security—against hunger and the fear of hunger, and against guilt and the fear of shame. So the final petition must also ask God for some kind of security based on faith in him. "And lead us not into temptation" does this perfectly. What it asks is that the King will lead us "in the right paths for his name's sake," to use the words of the twenty-third psalm. It asks God to lead us along trails on which we will not fear the bugaboo of temptation leaping out and waylaying us in the middle of the night. This petition cannot read "And lead us away from temptation," because that would be asking for too much. Temptation is a fact of everybody's life. The actual wording of the petition "And lead us not into temptation" expresses a more subtle and realistic idea. The temptation is still there in this petition, but we are protected from it by God's divine leadership. God leads us *through* temptation, unharmed. But we still have the freedom to grab a passing temptation and commit a sin.

What we do in Luke's last petition is ask God to lead us safely through all the spiritual shoals and undercurrents we may encounter. We ask him to lead us, *despite* all our temptation. But the petition cannot actually say "Lead us through temptation," because that would place the emphasis on the temptation, rather than on the leadership. What the petition really says, crudely put, is this: "Lead us by your grace—and, by the way, past temptation." Under God's tutelage, we want to mature spiritually, while we no longer fear the risk of sin, as decent people do, deep down, all their lives. This last petition relieves us of the distraction of spiritual anxiety as we search for the coming of the kingdom of God, with his leadership. After this petition, there are no anxieties left. We don't worry anymore about finding bread, we don't flagellate ourselves with guilt, and we no longer fear a spiritual disaster. We are finally free.

Other Visions

A body of scholars considers Jesus's prayer to be eschatological, that is to say, it deals with the last days of the world, the time when Jesus will return and destroy the forces of evil, that mysterious end time when the kingdom of God will finally come. The renowned Catholic scholar Raymond Brown says "The aorist tenses [in the original Greek] do not favor the interpretation of this petition in terms of daily deliverance from temptation." He then repeats some strained explanations of this last petition that have been offered by other scholars and saints over the years to get around the inference that God might actually lead us into temptation. "We can avoid these desperate interpretations, however," Father Brown says, "if we realize that we are not dealing with a question of daily temptation...but with the final battle between God and Satan." Father Brown then gives elegant scholarly arguments supporting this case, which partly turn on an alternative translation: "And do not lead us into trial." Finally, Brown presents this conclusion as being valuable to our daily prayers: "The return of Christ comes persistently closer each day…."The [Pater Noster] said as a fervent maranatha [entreaty to God] would not be an inappropriate welcome."[1]

The beauty of Jesus's prayer is that it is capable of many understandings, all of them true at the same time. And when Jesus gave this prayer to his disciples he didn't say: "These are the exact words you must always use. Don't ever depart from them." There is a sense in the gospels that he taught the disciples a strategy of prayer, not a formula. That's clear from Luke: "One of his disciples said to him 'Lord teach us [how] to pray, as John taught his disciples.' He said to them 'When you pray, say Father, etc.'" (Luke 11:1-2). Matthew also underlines the flexibility of Jesus's instructions. In his Gospel, Jesus says, "Pray then in this way: Our Father, etc." (Matthew 6:9). What Jesus imparts is an approach to prayer, though it's a focused approach within well-defined limits of language.

Therefore, many careful interpretations of this prayer can be true. The eschatological reading put forward by Father Brown is as valid as any of the others, but it cannot be the only approach because it would rob the prayer of its power in our spiritual lives today. The eschaton, or the second coming of Jesus, could be tomorrow morning. It could equally well be in ten thousand years' time. The Christian community has already waited two thousand years, and the second coming is not yet in sight. Armageddon, the final battle between good and evil, does not engage our concern today as we go about our daily spiritual struggles, big and small. In fact, most of us will probably be dead before the end time arrives. Insistence on the eschatological interpretation robs the prayer of its brilliance today and drives part of its spirituality into the future.

Millions of people claim this prayer as a blessing for today. And, aorist tense or not, the prayer has an internal consistency that confirms this approach. The last two petitions, for example—"Forgive us our sins" and "And lead us not into temptation"—are a linked theme which talks about going places, at first illegally, and then legally. The "trespass" for which we seek forgiveness is the offense of walking through a place where people must not go. Trespass is also a rejection of authority, the snubbing of a rightful leader who has made a just law about who may travel where and at what time. The next petition, "And lead us not into temptation," talks about the exact opposite of trespass. It asks for leadership off the privately-owned land onto the narrow path that leads legally through. We come out of our trespass with God's help and take the right path under his leadership. The first of these two petitions cannot be about forgiveness today, while the second is about the end time. That would be disjointed. Brown's interpretation is not the one that is the most valuable in our daily prayers.

But where are we actually going on that legal path as we bypass temptation? The Old Testament has many colorful tales of where God leads us, but they all end up in the same place—the kingdom of God. The nation of Israel was led out of the bondage of Egypt, which is emblematic of the prison of spiritual ignorance, and into the "land flowing with milk and honey," which is a symbol of the freedom and security of virtue. Jesus leads the new nation of Israel into God's kingdom and tells us exactly where that is. "The kingdom of God cometh not with observation: neither shall they say, Lo here! Or, lo there! For, behold, the kingdom of God is within you" (Luke 17:20-21, KJV). If the kingdom is here within you, then it must be the finest state of human nature, because it stands for close communion with God the King. Therefore, "And lead us not into temptation" asks that all of us be led away from debasement, which is where a person goes when he trespasses. It asks that God will lead us into the locus of the coming of the kingdom, where we can be true to our highest nature. This last petition says the kingdom of God is a living nation of liberated people.

The Living Fragments of the Kingdom

The petition matching "And lead us not into temptation" is "Thy kingdom come," which declares an important fact—God is human like us, because only a human being can be a king. The people of the world could be controlled by one of the three-fingered aliens depicted in H. G. Wells's *War of the Worlds,* but this creature could only ever be a dictator, never a king. A king is a member of the royal nation, elevated to rule by divine will and blessing. That's how the king derives his authority—from both his human origins among the people and his elevation by the grace of God. That's why "Thy kingdom come" insists that the divine King is a member of the human community, or to be more precise, the King's human subjects contain a spark of the King's divinity. But there are other reasons to believe that God is one of us and that his kingdom will unite a single human nation with its divinely human King. If we look here and there, we can see the fragments of God's human jigsaw puzzle—one that he has not yet assembled into a royal symphony of humanity and divinity, but clearly will.

The evidence for the possibility of the kingdom is that each place on Earth has its own living spiritual ethos that is built up from unique combinations of wildlife, rocks, and weather. These natural elements are assembled creatively in each place by the divine imagination to form what we might call a local art gallery of God. Each "garden of art" has its own wonders, such as snow leopards or grizzly bears or crystalline ice storms or shapely sand dunes. And each ethos, whether of tundra or jungle, encourages the local people to develop their own response to the creation and the Creator. Each band of people reflects this local ethos in a distinct language, culture, and art. And each vision of the divine is distinct from all the others. "What can there be in common," asks Northrop Frye, the great Canadian literary critic, "between an imagination nurtured on the Prairies, where it is a center of consciousness diffusing itself over a vast flat expanse stretching to the remote horizon, and one nurtured in British Columbia, where it is in the midst of gigantic trees and mountains leaping into the sky all around it, and obliterating the horizon everywhere?"[2] In some ancient civilizations, local cultures of dialect and art are noticeably different as little as twenty miles apart.

Who could ever comprehend a full reflection of God in all his infinite wholeness? That's why God organizes nature in such a way as to feed each one of us a vision of his character in a bite-sized piece, one that we are able to more easily digest. In North America, the natural scene exhibits more color than in, say, northern Europe, as if the birds and plants of the New World respond artistically to the more brilliant sunshine. The intense prettiness of the snow in North America inspires popular art that sparkles, which Britons find gaudy and childlike. The colors of the British Isles are deeper, as if to respond to the sky's more frequent overcast and rainy mood. Many North Americans come to dislike the heaviness of British taste, with its high content of toilet humor, not realizing that this is a British appreciation of the comic paradox of a spiritual being producing manure.

The British cherish originality and eccentricity. North Americans celebrate teamwork and efficiency—individuality is often held suspect. British eccentrics have produced many of history's great inventions, but have left them lying around instead of delivering them to popular usage. Americans are geniuses at marketing inventions widely, but not so much at inventing them. The two transatlantic peoples also have different notions of what is sacred. North Americans like to sanctify respectful human relations. The British accept more rigor in their conversations, and their sense of the sacred tends to be confined to church, the rights of property owners, and in former times, Empire. The distinctiveness of each culture even goes as far as to diverge on what usually constitutes upbeat thinking. In North America, people are encouraged to "think positive," which means to look at the present situation in the best possible light. In Britain, upbeat thinking often refers to "optimism," which admits that things may be rough right now, but will get better in the future.

Differences in the local ethos have produced the Irish love of education and the ability of the Maltese to absorb massive punishment without flinching. Russians revel in big things and indulge in a languorous melancholy. The Chinese love small things and produce pungent, impish art forms. These cultures are not created by any natural law. They are the aggregate tastes of all the people, the expression of the communal soul in the light of the world around it.

The reason for this myriad of cultures seems to be the opposite of the theology found in the Bible's legend of the Tower of Babel (Genesis 11:1-9). The tower got so high it supposedly alarmed God and prompted him to sow confusion among humankind by creating many tongues, and people could not understand one another. After God had done this, he supposedly felt less threatened by a tower with "its top in the heavens," knowing that the human builders could no longer communicate with one another and any further project must fail through confusion. But this legend appears to be upside down. God did not impose different languages on the races to divide and conquer them. Instead, God restored correct order. God is God and we are not, no matter how we try to reach such heights. God expresses his own nature joyfully, in different ways around the world, and these resonate within our human nature and come forth in many languages and cultures.

The world's thousands of cultures are the happy human response to God's playfulness, which is fed to us in tidbits, here and there. In moral people, the effect of this diversity is to encourage a sense of community, because each culture offers a fascination and an artistry and a new insight into God to all the people of all the other cultures. All these local visions of the divine, taken together, are an invitation from God to form a single, holy, worldwide community in which everybody learns to love the other and the King as in "Thy kingdom come." As all of us come together in the community of this world, we learn that if we act in unison, we have a greater vision of the mystery of God than any of us do separately. This loving embrace of the people of the world, one for the other, is the coming of the kingdom. All it needs for fulfillment is the coming of the King.

The Temptation to Destroy the Kingdom

Humans are inherently evil, according to some thinkers, such as the seventeenth century British philosopher Thomas Hobbes, who said we are all naturally selfish, violent, and lonely. "For the Lawes of Nature [including] ... doing to others as we would be done to, of themselves without the terrour of some Power, to cause them to be observed, are contrary to our naturall Passions, that carry us to Partiality, Pride, Revenge and the like."[3]

Humans are both good and bad to other thinkers, or more bad than good, or vice versa. This tedious debate about human moral ontology has gone on for ages without any clear resolution. In the end, it comes down to a question of optimism or pessimism, whether you see the good in human conduct or the bad, whether you are positive or negative, hopeful or despairing.

The Christian church has always taught that humanity is created good, and points to the sweeping growth of religious insight founded on God's revelation. We can also see for ourselves the way the human race rises above the blind laws of nature, even without divine revelation, solely on its own good values. No decent person, Christian or atheist, mates like animals do by choosing to marry the fittest person they can find so that their offspring will be strong and the race improved. Most people marry for love, which is the enduring cement of the kingdom of God, or they marry out of loyalty to their parents and community principles, converting it to love later. Handicapped people are not killed off or sequestered—except under a few ephemeral, evil regimes. Damaged people are allowed to deposit their genes in the gene pool through marriage, along with everybody else. And the offspring of diseased or handicapped people, such as the composer Ludwig van Beethoven, may reach the highest pinnacle of human achievement. If people were inherently evil, the moral condition of humanity would tend to deteriorate. But because humans are inherently good, the kingdom of God tends to be coming, with God's help and inspiration.

Temptation is the great, powerful urge of the individual to reverse the kingdom's coming into the kingdom's going, to scorn and batter the kingdom's potential citizens, one by one or en masse. We are tempted to hate blacks or whites or Bulgarians or ethnic Turks or women or dads. We want to rape, maim, kill, and plunder. Or we corrode society slowly by a little cheating or a little lying or a little affair. The source of these urges—temptation—arises directly out of our human nature, which is always trying to break free of the bonds we place around it for love's sake. Tired of discipline, eager to take life easy or to taste something exotic, we contemplate wrongdoing or crime. "Screw the kingdom of God, I want a holiday!" Or "I'm in charge here. I'll take what I want." Or "might is right, you prove it's not!" And every single person that was ever born of a woman is tempted.

Temptation is a wonderful companion and lots of fun, coming at one moment as a blazing passion, at another as a quiet fireside friend. It can be brazen as a trumpet or it can be subtle. It can be as quiet as a whisper or it can be sternly authoritative. It can test our true nature to the limit and harshly challenge the way we think we fit into society. And there's no escape hatch—for anybody. What we are tempted to do depends on how we have conditioned our lives up to that instant of temptation. As Teresa of Avila puts it in "The Interior Castle," temptation changes as a person moves among seven inner "dwelling-places" of prayer.[4] But there's always temptation. The less we pray, the more destructive our temptations.

To those who have no inner place of prayer, temptation can be brutal. In the early 1990s, a Toronto man named Paul Bernardo abducted two teenage girls with the help of his wife, Karla Homolka, and raped and sodomized them for weeks. He then murdered them and discarded the bodies as refuse. Bernardo acted out what people with even a smidgen of decency have absolutely no urge to do, even in their wildest dreams. We can only speculate that Bernardo and Homolka had very little spiritual life left within them. The Bernardos were excelled in evil by Jeffrey Dahmer, an American who murdered gay men, cannibalized them, and stored their uneaten body parts in a refrigerator for later consumption. The evil practiced by Dahmer and the Bernardos seems mysterious to the rest of us. But it is very easily explained. What distinguishes ordinary people from these monsters is that all of us, whether Christian, Buddhist, or atheist, fight little moral battles every day, perhaps against the urge to gossip or to steal or to lie or to form a destructive sexual liaison. We win most of these battles, often without realizing we have even fought them. The Bernardos of this world do not seem to fight any battles at all and sink into viler and viler temptations. As for us, we fight our little battles and win, and we move on. But we gain character all the time. And this war of wills never ends. When we have won the game at Level 2, we automatically graduate to Level 3 and Level 4. And the challenge can become much more subtle, but no less deadly.

The business economy, for example, is a fertile field for subtle temptation, as well as its opposite—unsung heroism. In the 1980s, a cheese factory in the hamlet of Alfred in southern Ontario won eight medals for its cheddar at the Royal Agricultural Winter Fair in Toronto. But the Alfred factory barely made a profit, year after year. When the owner was asked by a television producer why he didn't cut his costs, raise prices, and make some money, he replied irritably: "We're not in this business to make money. We're here to make cheese."[5] And the factory's cheddar—the only cheese it ever made—was among the finest in the world. The owner's ambition was not to become wealthy or to be noticed in the right circles. It was to serve the community in the one way that he knew he could.

The moral environment is more challenging for bigger businesses and presents more temptation. It may come in the name of science or the free market or the rights of the owners. Shareholders pester the executives of public companies to make as much money as they possibly can. "To hell with public service," they say. "The public doesn't own the shares. We do." And the managers jump.

Tycoons are seduced by the so-called law of supply and demand, which justifies high prices for scarce commodities, until only the wealthy can afford them. Such economic laws must be valid because they have been scientifically proven and are taught in the finest universities. But when you examine economics closely you discover that this so-called science is only an expression of the way the economy behaves when most people try to get as much money as they can out of it. What the law of supply and demand says is this: "People can charge more because people will pay more." Economics is a measure of greed, and like all science it ignores the deeper needs of our humanity. Few entrepreneurs give any thought to a lower price based on a moderate profit, to help the needy. That would mean the entrepreneur could not become a rich man or woman.

Economic temptation also presents itself in the guise of marketing theory or as the survival of the fittest or as a philosophy of the free market. A company sells a labeling machine and then charges a very high price for the only labels that fit the machine, because the machine's purchaser is trapped and must buy the company's labels, or waste the price of the machine itself. This pernicious practice must be okay, of course, because it's part of the high-level marketing techniques taught in colleges, where service to the community is not an issue. We are tempted to believe that these economic laws are like the law of gravity and are unbreakable, or come blessed with the highest authority and must be valid.

Temptation hits everybody. Police officers are hypnotized into protecting society from criminals by means of base falsehood. They tamper with evidence or ignore exonerating information in order to convict a person of murder because they *know in their hearts* he is guilty. This ugly, widespread phenomenon even has a name: noble cause corruption. Journalists face temptations to expose nonexistent wrongdoing and make themselves famous. In the 1970s, a journalist for the *Toronto Sun* wrote a damning exposé of an alleged crime committed by a Canadian cabinet minister that was based on pure invention. The journalist merely lusted for a reputation as an investigative reporter. He got one as a libeler. Other journalists succumb to more subtle temptations to shade the truth for political or other reasons.

Now and then we hear a whisper from our conscience, so we canvass the clergy for spiritual advice. But they, too, are tempted. And because of their status as spiritual leaders, they are much more likely to claim their tawdry actions are in God's service and therefore risk blasphemy. The 1982 war for the Falkland Islands between Britain and Argentina was declared morally right by the Catholic churches of both combatants, and each declared the other combatant wrong. In Argentina, the diocese of Buenos Aires was so convinced of its country's rectitude that it ceremonially blessed the weapons the Argentine soldiers would use to kill their British opponents. The temptation for these bishops and priests was to take pride in Argentina, right or wrong. What emerged later was that the Argentine junta invaded the Falkland Islands to distract mainland Argentines from the junta's abysmal economic failures at home. This is hardly a good reason for any church to bring God's blessing down on the instruments of death.

Temptation is often shadowy and deep. It embeds itself like a tick in the smallest crannies of the soul and becomes so much a part of oneself that it is hard to find and identify as a parasite. Temptation is the criminality of the subconscious trying to bring itself into the open in flashy clothing. It can lead to the unspeakable crime committed in the very heart of righteousness. Paul knew this well:

I do not even judge myself. I am not aware of anything against myself, but I am not thereby acquitted. It is the Lord who judges me. Therefore, do not pronounce judgment before the time, before the Lord comes, who will bring to light the things now hidden in darkness and will disclose the purposes of the heart. Then each one will receive commendation from God.
1 Corinthians 4:3-5

Temptation visits every man and woman that ever lived. Even Jesus was tempted—in the only way that God can be tempted—to play God. After the temptation to turn stones into bread,

> the devil took him to the holy city and placed him on the pinnacle of the temple, saying to him, "If you are the Son of God, throw yourself down; for it is written: 'He will command his angels concerning you' and 'On their hands they will bear you up, so that you will not dash your foot against a stone.'" Jesus said to him "Again it is written, 'Do not put the Lord your God to the test.'" Again the devil took him to a very high mountain and showed him all the kingdoms of the world and their splendor; and he said to him, "All these I will give you, if you will fall down and worship me." Jesus said to him "Away with you Satan! For it is written 'Worship the Lord your God and only serve him.'" Then the devil left him and suddenly angels came and waited on him. Matthew 4:3-11

The divine Jesus was tempted here in several ways. He was tempted to play God by using his powers selfishly for his own needs to make bread. He was tempted to taunt God the Father with a test of his love. And he was tempted to gain power by worshiping an idol, as so many of us are, even today. All human temptations are invitations to play God or worship idols, and in embracing them we abandon care for the coming of God's true kingdom. Perhaps the reason we can be tempted to play God is that we already have a spark of the divine within us. After all, animals do not engage in willfully destructive behavior. It takes a potential citizen of the kingdom to reject the kingdom and leave it. "And lead us not into temptation" becomes clearer. It is a petition that we be truly led by God, not by our delusions when we ape God.

Temptation, which is a call to do evil, is an essential part of the highest human spirituality, and strangely, a precursor to the coming of the kingdom. That's because temptation attaches itself to our freedom to reject God and harm others—or choose God and embrace others. Without that freedom to choose God, or reject him, there can be no love, because love is only ever a free choice and a free gift to the one who is loved. Love is never compelled. It can't be, or it is not love. And love is never the only choice laid before us. Love must be chosen over hatred. And if there is no love because there is no temptation to hate, there can be no triumphant kingdom of God because love is the kingdom's foundation. Temptation is the precursor to the kingdom of God, because if there were no temptation, there could be no kingdom of love.

And this last petition in Jesus's prayer becomes its glorious climax. It is far more beautiful than Psalm 23, which relies on mere pastoral images, lovely though they may be. What the final petition says is this: "Father! You define what is evil (we can't) and lead us through that minefield with love. Lead us constantly. Don't let us do anything to hurt you or ourselves. We are in your hands, and that's where we want to stay forever. Lead us into your kingdom—finally." Along with "Thy kingdom come," this is the ultimate prayer, in the sense of being the last thing that is ever said. These two petitions taken together, "Thy kingdom come" and "And lead us not into temptation," ask that the person and the community will always think of God, and that God will make himself known to the community and present himself in it, in all his glory, in the full flowering of the kingdom, which is the most glorious destiny of humankind. This is the most terrible of all prayers. It is nothing less than a prayer to gaze on the face of God.

9

The Power of the Prayer

Literature comes in a multitude of mindsets, each reflecting the spirituality of its age (or the lack thereof). Jesus's prayer is premodern, one might almost say pre-Christian. It harks back to the Stone Age, a time when words were believed to have a special power all of their own. By contrast, modern writing has little spiritual vigor and tends to be dominated by the conveyance of facts. This is true of science fiction, whodunits, do-it-yourself manuals, newspapers, even many novels. All of them convey ideas that are largely networks of data. Language is also used to convey, within a particular caste, information that is incomprehensible to the rest of us. "In benign nephrosclerosis proteinuria may be absent, intermittent, or moderate. The sediment contains only hyaline and finely granular casts,"[1] says *The Merck Manual of Diagnosis and Therapy,* in a line that is nonsense to everybody except doctors. The same trend is occurring in literary scholarship. As literature becomes more factitious and accessible to ordinary people, literary scholars are becoming an exclusive society, dealing in the arcane. The power of language is slipping from our grasp.

It was not always so. From 1000 to 1900, the English language went through a powerfully poetic phase. "Daffodils that come before the swallow dares, And take the winds of March with beauty,"[2] as Shakespeare wrote so exquisitely yet nonchalantly in *The Winter's Tale.* Fine language such as this helps us appreciate the loveliness of the world around us, beyond its content of conflict and information.

Further back, in the first century A.D., the writings of Paul were spiritually analytical and exhortatory of the good life, but also often beautiful. "Love is patient; love is kind; love is not envious or boastful or arrogant or rude. It does not insist on its own way; it is not irritable or resentful; it does not rejoice in wrongdoing, but rejoices in the truth" (1 Corinthians 13:4-6). These are words to comfort the soul.

Even further back, the Old Testament recognized the great power rooted in words and elevated language to a level close to the divine. "Then God said: 'Let there be light,' and there was light" (Genesis 1:3). This worship of words is echoed in the Gospel of John: "In the beginning was the Word and the Word was with God. And the Word was God" (John 1:1).

Jesus's prayer to the Father has the same power. The words are not merely spoken; they have the power to bring about great change, and always do. They move the human spirit toward God, in real time, and move God to bend down to us. The human heart is altered, often forever. And the prayer causes concrete change in the surrounding world. The person praying reaches his arms out to others and shares his bread and forgiveness with them. When all this happens, the actual world is altered—by the power of the prayer.

The prayer works this magic by taking the person praying into new lands of spiritual insight, and to a more concrete love of himself and all the people around him. This happens slowly, but inexorably.

The First Recitations

"Father" is a departure from the prison of solitude and fearful self-reliance toward an embrace of God and family. "Father" admits that success in the community does not flow from one's own talents, which are largely a divine gift anyway, but from God the Father whose designs for each of his children are loving beyond human comprehension. The person praying casts himself fearlessly into the arms of his Father. His faith allows him to walk on the water of God's love without fear of sinking into the drowning depths below.

"Hallowed be thy name" leaves the dreary prison of the self and a gnawing hunger for self-advancement, and asks that the whole world will recognize the Father's holiness, which means the power and grace of his love. This is a selfless prayer for God the Father himself—that he will receive his due recognition. It is also a prayer for the whole world, that it gain the glorious benefits of recognizing God's holiness. This petition is more than a conversion. It is an elevation.

"Thy kingdom come" is an abdication from one's own little padded throne. The person praying gives up all his comforting power over other people. He may still wield rightful authority in job or family, but he concedes that all power comes from God, and it must be exercised according to his will. "Thy kingdom come" admits—perhaps with courage—that God is the only true King.

"Give us this day our daily bread" gives up reliance on one's own resources in caring for one's self and family. God the Father is asked to provide just one day's ration of bread and all that that stands for. Each day's bread is prayed for in that day only, not just for one's self, but for all people everywhere. Life's necessities are no longer hoarded in the bank or in the attic to satisfy insecurity and greed. Instead, there is a humble faith that allows a person to reach past the inchoate dread that emanates from anonymous sources into a total reliance on God and the community.

"Forgive us our sins, we too forgive all those who trespass against us" is an abdication from the hardness of heart that refuses to admit one's own wrongdoing while at the same time cruelly condemning the actions of others. This prayer corrects both defects, which are essentially the same. It asks for mercy and recognizes that we must show mercy to others, just like God the Father. Society changes radically when we embrace this worldview.

"And lead us not into temptation" is an abdication from self-righteousness. We often court evil in the belief that we are making good moral judgments out of our own unarguable authority. Or we delude ourselves that what we did wrong was actually right. Our motivation is always pride, rather than an ear for the voice of God. "And lead us not into temptation" means "come and lead us truly, rather than only apparently. Take our hands and lead us into the kingdom, for we cannot rely on our own understanding of right and wrong."

Jesus's Prayer Delivers Freedom

The adventurer in search of the kingdom always speaks the same words when he says Jesus's prayer, but he or she enters new territory every time. The symphony of faith that accompanies him moves from a lovely largo, with all its haunting memories of worldly sorrow, into a faster spiritual andante that shakes off all the shadows.

"Father" brings freedom from the solitude of independence to an everlasting belonging to God the Father and the worldwide family of brothers and sisters.

"Hallowed be thy name" brings liberation out of the smallness of a worldly man or woman into the enveloping greatness of a holy God and his nation.

"Thy kingdom come" frees the person praying from the tyranny of a Godless self-rule and makes him or her free to be divinely ruled.

"Give us this day our daily bread" brings freedom from the anxiety of yesterday and tomorrow into the total security of today.

"Forgive us our sins, we too forgive all those who trespass against us" brings liberation from the dungeon of guilt and the burden of criticizing other people's wrongdoing into the soaring weightlessness of reconciliation.

"And lead us not into temptation" brings freedom from the fear of falling off the cliff and from the exhausting need to play God in the lives of others.

Jesus's Prayer Opens the Soul to Joy

"Father" is a proclamation of the joy of childlike innocence.

"Hallowed be thy name" receives the joy of holiness spilling over from God's abundance.

"Thy kingdom come" celebrates the towering joy of God's majesty, finally made known.

"Give us this day our daily bread" captures the elusive joy of material things as a free gift and not a conquest.

"Forgive us our sins, we too forgive all those who trespass against us" finds the joy of everlasting peace with God and the world.

"And lead us not into temptation" establishes the eternal joy of spiritual security.

The person saying this prayer is liberated from the troubles of the world—even sometimes from bad health—and enters into a much happier and more joyous state. As he does so, he powerfully influences all the people around him for the better by radiating peace and confidence. It's like a pebble being thrown into a pond. Waves spread out over the pond quite far away from the point of impact. In this case, with the grace of God, in answer to this one person's prayer, the healing ripples spread out farther than his immediate circle, even—a little—to the farthest reaches of the globe, helping to bind the community together, and bring about the coming of the kingdom of God.

Notes

Chapter One: The Prayer

1. This book is a work of reflection on what is prayed with devotion by the greatest number of people. For that reason, the version of Luke's prayer that is used throughout the text (and as chapter headings) comes from the New Testament translation by Msgr R. A. Knox, which was authorized by the Roman Catholic Hierarchy of England and Wales and published as A Chanticleer Edition by Sheed & Ward, 1946. This version was chosen because its language is similar to the prayer that is spoken and loved all over the world today, even though the use of "thy" is archaic.

Unless otherwise indicated, all Biblical quotations in the narrative are from the NRSV translation. The notation KJV indicates King James Version.

2. Hilda C. Graef, trans., *St. Gregory of Nyssa: The Lord's Prayer* (London: Longmans Green & Co., 1954).

3. Leonardo Boff, *The Lord's Prayer* (Maryknoll, NY: Orbis Books, 1983).

4. Ezra Pound, *How to Read* (New York: Haskell House Publishers Ltd., 1971), p. 21.

5. John Henry Cardinal Newman, *Tracts Theological and Ecclesiastical* (London: Longmans Green & Co., 1895), p. 158.

6. Here are Julian of Norwich's actual quotes: "The Second Person of the Trinity is our mother in nature, in our substantial making. In him we are grounded and rooted, and he is our mother by mercy in our sensuality, by taking flesh."

"Thus our mother, Christ, in whom our parts are kept unseparated, works in us in various ways. For in our mother, Christ, we profit and increase, and in mercy he reforms and restores us, and by virtue of his passion, death, and resurrection joins us to our substance. This is how our mother, Christ, works in mercy in all his beloved children who are submissive and obedient to him." *Revelations of Divine Love of Julian of Norwich*, M. L. Del Mastro, trans. (New York: Doubleday, 1977).

7. Miles Harvey, *The Island of Lost Maps* (New York: Random House, 2000), p. 262.

8. Joseph Campbell, *The Hero with a Thousand Faces* (Princeton, N.J.: Princeton University Press, 1949), pp. 69, 71.

9. Swami Vivekananda, a twentieth century Hindu sage, *Vivekananda, The Yogas and Other Works* (New York: Ramakrishna-Vivekananda Center, 1953), p. 206.

Chapter Two: Father

1. "Burnt Norton Part II," in *T. S. Eliot: Four Quartets*, eds. (London: Faber and Faber, 1959), page 15.

2. John A. Hardon S.J., *The Question and Answer Catholic Catechism* (Garden City, N.Y.: Image Books, 1981), p. 25.

3. The Most Rev. M. Sheehan, Archbishop of Germia, *Apologetics and Catholic Doctrine* (Dublin: M. H. Gill and Son Ltd., 1953), pp. 60, 66.

4. William Shakespeare, *Macbeth*, 5.5.24-28.

5. J. W. Grant MacEwen, *Portraits from the Plains* (Toronto: McGraw Hill Co. of Canada Ltd., 1971), p. 90.

6. William Barclay, *The Lord's Prayer* (Louisville: Westminster John Knox Press, 1998), p. 30. The quote comes from Hardy's work, *The Dynasts*.

7. G. K. Chesterton, *The Victorian Age in Literature* (London: Williams and Norgate, n.d.), p. 143.

8. "The Lotos-Eaters," *Poems of Lord Alfred Tennyson*, eds. (Oxford: Oxford University Press, 1950), p. 27.

9. *Dying We Live* (London: Fontana Books (Collins), 1958), p. 81.

10. Ibid., p. 83.

11. Francis, Duke of La Rochefoucauld, *Reflections or Sentences and Moral Maxims* (New York: William Gowans, 1851), No. 376, p. 109.

12. News reports April 30, 2001, Kansas City.

13. *The Rubaiyat of Omar Khayyam*, Edward Fitzgerald translation, fourth edition, 3.64.

14. From newspaper reports, recently confirmed with Dr. Elmasry.

15. Figures reported in Robert Harrris, *Archangel* (New York: Random House, 1998), p. 137.

16. The man who checked himself out of a hospital room was Norman Cousins.

Chapter Three: Hallowed Be Thy Name

1. Karen Armstrong, *A History of God* (New York: Ballantine Books, 1993), p. 356.

2. Herodotus, *The Histories* (Penguin Classics) (London: Penguin, 1954), p. 94.

3. Stephan and Norbert Lebert, *My Father's Keeper: Children of Nazi Leaders— An Intimate History of Damage and Denial* (New York: Little, Brown & Co., 2001), p. 112.

4. Abram Leon Sachar, *A History of the Jews* (New York: Alfred A. Knopf, 1948), p. 35.

5. Jonathan Kirsch, *King David* (New York: Ballantine Books, 2000), p. 1.

6. *A History of the Jews*, p. 34.

7. Martin Middlebrook, *The Fight for the Malvinas* (London: Penguin Books Ltd., 1990), pp. 185-186.

Chapter Four: Thy Kingdom Come

1. Letter to M. Creighton, Appendix, *Historical Essays and Studies,* (London: MacMillan & Co., Ltd., 1908), p. 504.

2. Commentary in the *National Post,* December 21, 2003.

3. Winston Churchill, Speech in the House of Commons, November 11, 1947, quoted in eds. *Chambers Dictionary of Quotations* (Edinburgh: Chambers Harrap Publishers, Ltd., 1996), p. 265, entry 32.

4. *The Histories,* pp. 490-494. The translation of the inscription is taken from Steven Pressfield, *Gates of Fire* (New York: Doubleday, 1998).

5. Well-known remarks made during the London blitz, April 1940, and reprinted on the death of the Queen Mother, April 1, 2002.

6. Ernle Bradford, *The Mighty Hood* (London: Hodder and Stoughton, 1959). See also Cajus Bekker, *Hitler's Naval War* (New York: Kensington Publishing Corp., 1974) and Cecil King, *Rule Britannia* (London: The Studio Publications, 1941).

7. The facts are taken from Internet sources and John F. Kennedy in *Profiles of Courage* (New York: Harper and Row Publishers, 1964).

8. *Profiles of Courage,* p. 119.

9. Ibid., p. 122.

10. Ibid., p. 111.

11. Ann Wroe, *Pontius Pilate: The Biography of an Invented Man* (London: Jonathan Cape, 1999), p. 60.

12. *Profiles of Courage*, p. 124.

13. The facts are taken entirely from a *Globe and Mail* newspaper clipping dated September 5, 1991.

14. The story of Afghan resistance to the Russians is from newspaper reports of the mid-1980s.

Chapter Six: Give Us This Day Our Daily Bread

1. K. C. Cole, *The Hole in the Universe* (New York: Harcourt Inc., 2001), pp. 169-170.

2. Robert Jastrow, *God and the Astronomers* (New York: W. W. Norton & Co. Inc., 1992), p. 107.

3. *The Hole in the Universe*, p. 65.

4. The Siege of Malta is described in various sources, including F. S. De Domenico, *An Island Beleaguered* (Malta: Giov. Muscat, 1946); Ernle Bradford, *Siege: Malta 1940–1943* (London: Hamish Hamilton Ltd., 1985); and Lord James Douglas-Hamilton M. P., *The Air Battle for Malta* (Edinburgh: Mainstream Publishing Company Ltd., 1981).

5. Ernle Bradford, *Siege: Malta 1940–1944* (London: Hamish Hamilton, 1985) p. 555.

6. Winston S. Churchill, *The Hinge of Fate* (Boston: Houghton, Mifflin & Co., 1950), p. 506.

7. Nicholas Monsarrat, *The Kappillan of Malta* (London: Cassell & Co., 1973), p. 396.

8. Immanuel Velikovsky, *Worlds in Collision* (New York: Doubleday & Co., 1950), pp. 134-138.

9. Farley Mowat, *The Grey Seas Under* (Boston: Little Brown & Co., 1958), p. 38.

Chapter Seven: And Forgive Us Our Sins; We Too Forgive All Those Who Trespass Against Us

1. G. K. Chesterton, *The Ballad of the White Horse* (London: Methuen & Co., 1921), p. 21.

2. Gilbert K. Chesterton, *Orthodoxy* (London: The Bodley Head, 1908), p. 93.

3. Rabindranath Tagore, *Gitanjali* (London: MacMillan & Co. Ltd., 1915), p. 88.

4. Kathryn Watterson, *Not by the Sword* (New York: Simon & Schuster, 1995). The Larry Trapp quote is from p. 153.

Chapter Eight: And Lead Us Not into Temptation

1. Raymond E. Brown, S. S., "The Pater Noster as an Eschatological Prayer," *Theological Studies*, vol. 22 (June 1961): 175.
2. Northrop Frye, *The Bush Garden* (Toronto: House of Anansi Press, 1971), p. ii.
3. C. B. Macpherson, ed., *Hobbes Leviathan* (Pelican Classics) (New York: Penguin Books, 1968), p. 223.
4. Kieran Kavanaugh, *Teresa of Avila: The Interior Castle* (The Classics of Western Spirituality) (New York: Paulist Press, 1979), pp. 49-50, 58, 60, 68, 87, 108, 182.
5. Conversation with the author, 1991.

Chapter Nine: The Power of the Prayer

1. Editor(s), *The Merck Manual of Diagnosis and Therapy*, 12th edition, (Essex, United Kingdom: Merck Sharp & Dohme Research Laboratories, 1972), p. 619.
2. William Shakespeare, *The Winter's Tale*, edition 4.4.118-120.

OTHER RESOURCES FROM AUGSBURG

Awed to Heaven, Rooted in Earth by Walter Brueggemann
192 pages, 0-8006-3460-8

This thoughtful collection of prayers emerged from Brueggemann's thirty-five years of teaching in seminaries. Full of reflection, faith, and dialogue, they reveal another side of this gifted author from what his many readers are accustomed to.

What Can Happen When We Pray by Jeremiah A. Wright Jr.
384 pages, 0-8066-3406-5

A year-round daily devotional that proclaims that standing on the promises of God is the best place to be. This book is organized with daily prayers and reflections, as well as song suggestions and journal space to reinforce each day's lessons.

A Beginner's Guide to Prayer by Richard J. Beckman
110 pages, 0-8066-2674-7

This book looks at the rhythms of the prayer life, the sense of God's absence and presence, the Holy Spirit and prayer, the language we use, and the Lord's Prayer. Within this book are woven Jesus's practice and teaching about prayer, other biblical examples, and experiences of people today.

Keeping Company with Jesus by Jackie L. Smallbones
112 pages, 0-8066-5157-1

Revisits Gospel stories of Jesus's interaction with individuals dealing with terrible hardships. The author draws from difficulties in today's society, such as breast cancer and unemployment, and uses Gospel stories to provide spiritual encouragement to people in those situations.

Available wherever books are sold.